The Ultimate Amazon Web Services Guide From Beginners to Advanced

JEFFREY CLOUD

Additionally, the information in the following pages is intended only for informational purposes and should thus be thought of as universal. As befitting its nature, it is presented without assurance regarding its prolonged validity or interim quality. Trademarks that are mentioned are done without written consent and can in no way be considered an endorsement from the trademark holder.

Disclaimer Notice:

Please note the information contained within this document is for educational and entertainment purposes only. All effort has been executed to present accurate, up to date, and reliable, complete information. No warranties of any kind are declared or implied. Readers acknowledge that the author is not engaging in the rendering of legal, financial, medical or professional advice. The content within this book has been derived from various sources. Please consult a licensed professional before attempting any techniques outlined in this book.

By reading this document, the reader agrees that under no circumstances is the author responsible for any losses, direct or indirect, which are incurred as a result of the use of information contained within this document, including, but not limited to, — errors, omissions, or inaccuracies.

Table of Contents

7

Chapter # 1

Origin:

Amazon Web Services (AWS) was propelled by the web-based business giant Amazon in 2006, rapidly developing into an organization that has essentially changed the IT business in a time of far-reaching distributed computing and cut out a market-driving position.

Collaboration Research Group's figures in 2018 peg AWS as the reasonable market pioneer all-inclusive for open IaaS and PaaS administration incomes, at 40 percent share in the market, trailed by Microsoft at 17 percent, Google at 8 percent and Alibaba at 5 percent.

In any case, Microsoft and Google have expanded their attention on open cloud in current years, and present a crucial threat to AWS as huge organizations think about how to move more outstanding tasks at hand out of the data center.

Simultaneously, cloud take-up is thought of in certain quarters to in any case especially be in its outset -

Gartner, for one, predicts the overall IaaS market to develop to $71.5 billion by 2020, so there is a lot of markets to go around.

Development:

In this report, "development and test" alludes to the different tools and practices applied when developing the software. Despite the kind of software to be built up, an appropriate arrangement of advancement and test rehearses is key to progress. In any case, developing applications requires software engineers, yet in addition IT assets, which are dependent upon some crucial constraints like time, cash, and aptitude. The product life cycle commonly comprises of the accompanying primary components: This whitepaper covers parts of the development.

The AWS Cloud Development Kit (AWS CDK) is an open-source programming development system to demonstrate and arrangement your cloud application assets utilizing well-known programming languages.

Provisioning cloud applications can be a difficult procedure that expects you to perform manual activities, compose custom contents, maintain templates, or learn area explicit languages. AWS CDK utilizes the nature and expressive intensity of programming languages for demonstrating your applications. It gives you high-level segments that preconfigure cloud assets with demonstrated defaults, so you can manufacture cloud applications without waiting to be a specialist. AWS CDK arrangements your assets in a safe, repeatable way through AWS CloudFormation. It also empowers you to make and share your very own custom parts that incorporate your association's necessities, helping you start new projects quicker.

Utilizing AWS, you can demand figure power, storage, and different administrations in minutes and have the adaptability to pick the development stage or programming model that makes well for the issues they're attempting to solve. You pay just for what you use, with no direct costs or long-term duties, making AWS a practical method to convey applications. Here are some of the instances of how associations, from examining firms to enormous enterprises, use

AWS today:

A major organization rapidly and economically sends new inside applications, for example, HR arrangements, finance applications, inventory administration arrangements, and web-based preparing to its distributed workforce.

An e-commerce business site obliges unexpected interest for a "hot" item brought about by viral buzz from Facebook and Twitter without updating its foundation.

A pharmaceutical research firm executes enormous scale simulations utilizing processing power gave by AWS. Media organizations serve boundless video, music, and other media to their overall client base.

AWS takes out both the requirement for expensive equipment and the management pain that goes with owning and working it. Owning equipment and IT framework generally includes a capital consumption for a 3—5 year time span, where most improvement and test groups need register or capacity for a considerable length of time, days, weeks, or months. This distinction in timescales can cause grating because of the trouble for IT activities to fulfill synchronous solicitations from project groups, even as they are constrained by a fixed arrangement of assets. The outcome is that project groups invest a ton of energy in legitimizing, sourcing, and holding assets. This time could be spent concentrating on the primary current task.

Developers fundamentally utilize their local PCs or work areas to run their improvement environments. This is normally where the IDE is introduced, where unit tests are run, where source code is checked in, and so forth. However, there are also a couple of situations where on-request development conditions facilitated in AWS are useful. Some development projects may utilize specific arrangements of tools where it would be unwieldy or asset concentrated to introduce and keep up these on local machines, particularly if such instruments are utilized rarely. For such cases, you can plan and arrange advancement situations with required devices (improvement tools, source control, unit test suites, IDEs, and so on.).

Chapter # 2

What is Aws?

Amazon Web Services (AWS) is the world's generally extensive and comprehensively received cloud stage, offering more than 165 completely highlighted administrations from data centers universally. A large number of clients, including the quickest developing new businesses, major projects and driving government organizations trust AWS to control their framework, become progressively agile, and lower costs.

Growth of AWS:

Amazon Web Services (AWS) kept on being the superstar, becoming 37% in deals to $8.4 billion. That growth figure is the principal sub-40% development rate since Amazon began breaking out AWS numbers. In any case, AWS still represented about 13% of Amazon's complete income for the quarter. AWS is the distributed computing market pioneer, in front of Microsoft Azure and Google Cloud.

Membership administrations were up 37% to $4.7 billion. That would principally establish Amazon Prime, which the organization is growing to offer arrangements at places like Whole Foods.

Amazon's "other" class, which generally covers the organization's publicizing business, was incidentally additionally up 37% to $3 billion in income. The organization thinks bounty about what its clients need to purchase, or even don't have any desire to purchase, and it's increasingly utilizing that for its publicizing business.

"Clients are reacting to Prime's move to one-day delivery, we've gotten a great deal of positive criticism and seen quickening sales growth,"

Amazon CEO Jeff Bezos said in an announcement. "Free one-day delivery is currently accessible to Prime individuals on in excess of 10 million things, and we're simply beginning. A major thank you to the group for proceeding to make life simpler for clients."

Bezos obviously needed to concentrate on Prime Day, which has been a massive accomplishment for the organization. Prime Day, which really falls in Amazon's second from last quarter, was indeed the biggest shopping occasion in Amazon history, and this year deals from the two-day occasion (July 15 and July 16) outperformed the past Black Friday and Cyber Monday joined. The two days were also the greatest ever for part information exchanges.

Potential:

Since AWS's expense is adjusted depending on the clients' utilization, new businesses and independent companies can see the undeniable advantages of utilizing Amazon for their processing needs. Indeed, AWS is incredible for building a business from the base as it gives every one of the instruments important to organizations to fire up with the cloud. For existing organizations, Amazon gives low-cost migration services with the goal that your current foundation can be consistently moved over to AWS.

As an organization develops, AWS gives assets to help in extension and as the plan of action takes into account adaptable use, clients will never need to invest energy pondering whether they have to reconsider their registering use. Actually, besides budgetary reasons, organizations could sensibly "set and forget" all their processing needs.

Seemingly, AWS is considerably more secure than an organization facilitating its own site or capacity. AWS presently has many server farms over the globe which are continuously observed and carefully kept up. The broadening of the data centers guarantees that a disaster striking one area doesn't cause permanent information loss around the world. Envision if Netflix somehow happened to have the entirety of their staff documents, their substance and their upheld up information unified nearby on the eve of a tropical storm. It would be madness.

In fact, in any event, failing a natural disaster, restricting information in an effectively recognizable area and where several individuals can practically get to is unwise. AWS has attempted to keep their data centers as covered up as could be expected under the circumstances, finding them in out-of-the-way areas and permitting access just on a fundamental basis. The data centers and every one of the information contained in that are protected from interruptions and, with Amazon's involvement with cloud administrations, blackouts and potential attacks can be immediately distinguished and effectively cured, 24 hours per day. The equivalent can't be said for a little organization whose registering is dealt with by a single IT fellow working out of a huge office.

AWS is a cash cow for Amazon. The administrations are shaking up the figuring scene similarly that Amazon is changing America's retail space. By estimating its cloud items very inexpensively, Amazon can give moderate and scalable services to everybody from the most current beginning up to a Fortune 500 organization.

Chapter # 3

Terminology:

One of the most well-known suppliers is Amazon Web Services (AWS), and many working in IT are required to get personally familiar with the innovation. However, the ambush of AWS terminology and the confusion regarding why everything is prefixed with "cloud" or "elastic" can be somewhat overpowering. To help, here's a glossary-style cheat sheet with regular terms and expressions you'll seem to be you plunge further into the universe of distributed computing.

Normal AWS Terms

AWS IoT: AWS IoT is an overseen cloud administration that lets associated devices effectively and safely communicate with cloud applications and different gadgets.

Certificate Manager: AWS Certificate Manager lets you effectively arrangement, manage, and convey Secure Sockets Layer/Transport Layer Security (SSL/TLS) certificates for use with AWS administrations.

CloudFormation: AWS CloudFormation allows you to make and update an assortment of related AWS assets in a predictable manner.

CloudFront: Amazon CloudFront gives an approach to distribute substance to end-clients with low inactivity and high information move speeds.

CloudSearch: AWS CloudSearch is a completely overseen scan administration for sites and applications.

CloudTrail: AWS CloudTrail gives expanded perceivability into client action by recording API calls made for you.

Data Pipeline: AWS Data Pipeline is a lightweight orchestration administration for occasional, information-driven work processes.

DMS: AWS Database Migration Service (DMS) encourages you to move databases to the cloud effectively and safely while limiting personal time.

DynamoDB: Amazon DynamoDB is a scalable NoSQL information store that oversees distributed copies of your information for high availability.

EC2: Amazon Elastic Compute Cloud (EC2) gives resizable process limit in the cloud.

EC2 Container Service: Amazon ECS enables you to effortlessly run and oversee Docker compartments over a bunch of Amazon EC2 occasions.

Flexible Beanstalk: AWS Elastic Beanstalk is an application holder for sending and overseeing applications.

ElastiCache: Amazon ElastiCache improves application performance by enabling you to recover information from an in-memory storing framework.

Flexible File System: Amazon Elastic File System (Amazon EFS) is a file storage administration for Amazon Elastic Compute Cloud (Amazon EC2) occurrences.

Elasticsearch Service: Amazon Elasticsearch Service is an overseen administration that makes it simple to convey, work, and scale Elasticsearch, a prominent open-source search and analytics engine.

Elastic Transcoder: Amazon Elastic Transcoder gives you a chance to change over your media documents in the cloud effectively, requiring little to no effort, and at scale.

EMR: Amazon Elastic MapReduce gives you a chance to perform enormous information assignments, for example, web ordering, information mining, and log document examination.

Glacier: Amazon Glacier is a low-cost storage administration that gives secure and tough storage to information archiving and backup.

IAM: AWS Identity and Access Management (IAM) lets you safely control access to AWS administrations and assets.

Inspector: Amazon Inspector empowers you to break down the behavior of the applications you run in AWS and causes you to distinguish potential security issues.

Kinesis: Amazon Kinesis administrations make it simple to work with constant spilling information in the AWS cloud.

Lambda: AWS Lambda is a figure administration that runs your code because of occasions and automatically deals with the compute assets for you.

Machine Learning: Amazon Machine Learning is the help that empowers you to effortlessly construct smart applications.

OpsWorks: AWS OpsWorks is a DevOps stage for overseeing applications of any scale or complexity on the AWS cloud.

RDS: Amazon Relational Database Service (RDS) makes it simple to set up, work, and scale recognizable social databases in the cloud.

Redshift: Amazon Redshift is a quick, completely oversaw, petabyte-scale information stockroom that makes it cost-effective to dissect every one of your information utilizing your current business intelligence tools.

Route 53: Amazon Route 53 is an adaptable and exceptionally accessible Domain Name System (DNS) and Domain Name Registration administration.

SES: Amazon Simple Email Service (SES) empowers you to send and get an email.

SNS: Amazon Simple Notification Service (SNS) gives you a chance to distribute messages to subscribers or different applications.

Storage Gateway: AWS Storage Gateway safely incorporates on-premises IT environments with distributed storage for reinforcement and disaster recovery.

SQS: Amazon Simple Queue Service (SQS) offers a solid, highly scalable, facilitated line for putting away messages.

SWF: Amazon Simple Workflow (SWF) coordinates the entirety of the processing steps inside an application.

S3: Amazon Simple Storage Service (S3) can be utilized to store and recover any measure of information.

VPC: Amazon Virtual Private Cloud (VPC) gives you a chance to dispatch AWS assets in a private, segregated cloud.

Chapter # 4

Where amazon web services operate?

AWS serves over a million dynamic clients in excess of 190 nations. We are consistently growing worldwide framework to enable our clients to accomplish lower inactivity and higher throughput, and to guarantee that their information dwells just in the AWS Region they determine. As our clients develop their organizations, AWS will keep on giving the foundation that meets their worldwide requirements.

The AWS Cloud framework is worked around AWS Regions and Availability Zones. An AWS Region is a physical area on the planet where we have different Availability Zones. These Availability Zones offer you the capacity to work generation applications and databases that are all the more highly accessible, fault-tolerant, and scalable than would be conceivable from a solitary server farm. The AWS Cloud works in more than 60 Availability Zones inside more than 20 geographic Regions around the globe, with reported designs for greater Availability Zones and Regions. For more data on the AWS Cloud Availability Zones and AWS Regions, see AWS Global Infrastructure. Every Amazon Region is intended to be totally isolated from the other Amazon Regions. This accomplishes the best conceivable adaptation to non-critical failure and strength. Every Availability Zone is isolated, yet the Availability Zones in a Region are associated through low-latency joins. AWS gives you the adaptability to put examples and store information inside numerous geographic locales just as over various Availability Zones inside each AWS Region. Every Availability Zone is structured as an autonomous failure zone. This means Availability Zones are physically isolated inside a common metropolitan locale and are situated in lower chance flood fields (explicit flood zone order shifts by AWS Region). Moreover, discrete uninterruptable power supply (UPS) and on-location reinforcement age offices, they are each sustained through various matrices from free utilities to additionally lessen single purposes of failure. Accessibility Zones are for the most part redundantly associated with different level 1 travel suppliers.

AWS Partner Network?

The AWS Partner Network (APN) is the worldwide partner program for innovation and counseling organizations that influence Amazon Web Services to fabricate arrangements and administrations for clients. The APN enables organizations to assemble, market, and sell their AWS contributions by giving significant business, specialized, and marketing support.

There are a huge number of APN Partners from all over the world. Over 90% of Fortune 100 organizations and most of Fortune 500 organizations use APN Partner arrangements and administrations.

Work with an APN Partner

The APN encourages you to distinguish and pick great APN Partners with high-quality AWS skills, remarkably situated to help your organization at any phase of your Cloud Adoption Journey.

Become an APN Partner

Regardless of whether you are starting to build your business or extending your training on AWS, the APN is an incredible spot to begin. Join at no cost and advance your APN Partner journey with AWS.

Grow as an APN Partner

As an APN Partner you will separate your business, arrive at new clients quicker, and deeply engage in with existing clients by utilizing various APN Partner Programs.

AWS Marketplace?

AWS Marketplace is a curated advanced index that makes it simple for clients to discover, purchase, convey, and oversee outsider programming and administrations that clients need to manufacture arrangements and maintain their organizations. AWS Marketplace incorporates a huge number of programming listings from well-known classifications, for example, security, organizing, capacity, AI, business knowledge, database, and DevOps. AWS Marketplace also rearranges software authorizing and procurement with adaptable estimating alternatives and numerous arrangement strategies.

Clients can rapidly dispatch pre-arranged software with only a couple of clicks, and pick programming arrangements in AMI and SaaS groups, just as different configurations. Adaptable estimating choices incorporate free trial, hourly, month to month, yearly, multi-year, and BYOL, and get charged from one source. AWS handles charging and installments, and programming charges show up on clients' AWS bill.

You use AWS Marketplace as a subscriber (purchaser) or as a supplier (vendor), or both. Anybody with an AWS record can utilize AWS Marketplace as a purchaser and can enlist to turn into a supplier. A supplier can be an independent software vendor (ISV), esteem included affiliate or person that has something to offer that works with AWS items and administrations.

Each item on AWS Marketplace has experienced a curation procedure. On the item page, there can be at least one contribution to the item. At the point when the supplier presents an item in AWS Marketplace, they characterize the cost of the item and the terms and states of utilization. At the point when a consumer subscribes into an item offering, they consent to the evaluating, and terms and conditions set for the offer.

Chapter # 5

How AWS works

AWS is isolated into various administrations and each can be designed in various manners dependent on the client's needs. Clients should have the option to see configuration choices and individual server maps for an AWS administration.

More than 100 administrations involve the Amazon Web Services portfolio, including those for the process, databases, framework the executives, application improvement and security. These administrations, by class, include:

- Information Management

- Compute

- Hybrid cloud

- Capacity databases

- Management

- Relocation

- Networking

- Monitoring

- Governance

- Security

- Development tools

- Artificial intelligence (AI)

- Big data management

- Mobile development

- Messages and notification

- Analytics

Availability

Amazon Web Services gives administrations from many data centers spread crosswise over accessibility zones (AZs) in areas over the world. An AZ speaks to an area that ordinarily contains various physical data centers, while a district is a variety of AZs in geographic proximity associated with low-latency network links.

A business will pick one or numerous accessibility zones for a variety of reasons, for example, consistency and proximity to end clients.

Storage

Amazon Simple Storage Service (S3) gives adaptable article storage for data reinforcement, authentic and investigation. An IT proficient stores information and documents as S3 objects, which can run up to 5 GB, inside S3 buckets to keep them sorted out. A business can set aside cash with S3 through its Infrequent Access storage tier or use Amazon Glacier for long-term cold storage.

Databases, data management

The Amazon Relational Database Service which incorporates choices for Oracle, SQL Server, PostgreSQL, MySQL, MariaDB and a restrictive high-performance database called Amazon Aurora gives a social database management system for AWS clients. AWS additionally offers oversaw NoSQL databases through Amazon DynamoDB.

Best AWS Features

Amazon Web Services has different features that make it strong among various firms. A portion of the features of AWS are:-

Mobile-Friendly Access

Mobile friendly access incorporates two different ways:-

I. AWS Mobile Hub

This Amazon Web Services include is for both Android and IOS. AWS Mobile Hub supports and guides you towards a reasonable and good component for your application. It incorporates a console that encourages you to get to AWS services that incorporate advancement, testing, and observing of the mobile application. It incorporates clear approaches to choose and arrange mobile application features like content delivery and message pop-ups.

ii. AWS Mobile SDK

By this AWS feature, your application can simply access to Amazon Web Services, for example, Dynamo DB, S3, and Lambda. The Mobile SDK supports IOS, Android, Web, React Native, Unity and some more.

b. Serverless Cloud Functions

Amazon API and Amazon Gateway help clients by running their code and scaling it. The main thing a client needs to do is to upload the code with the assistance of a cell phone. Clients should not deal with the servers as the entire procedure is then overseen by AWS. Applications that are made need to deliver an incredible experience to the clients. We need numerous tasks to be performed on the double and for that, we need back-end code that runs and reacts to the code. Dealing with the foundation to have back-end codes requires size, arrangement and lots of servers. AWS Serverless cloud work helps the client so that they should concentrate just on building the application. Server the board is finished by AWS alongside it, it performs scaling, fixing and administration of the infrastructure.

c. Databases

Amazon gives a database according to your requirements and the database gave by them is totally overseen by them. A portion of the databases and their uses are:

I. Relational Database-Transactional Purposes.

ii. Non-Relational Database – Internet-Scale Applications.

iii. Data Warehouse-Analytics.

iv. In-memory data Store-Caching and Real-time workloads

v. Graph Database-Application with exceptionally associated information.

Storage

It is one of the AWS features, given by Amazon is efficient, adaptable and simple to utilize. The capacity gave by AWS can utilize freely just as in combination to meet your necessity. The following are the kinds of capacity given by AWS.

- Amazon glacier-It is utilized for long-term storage.

- Amazon Simple Storage Service-It gives scalable item storage to documented, examination and data backup.

- The Amazon EBS-It gives block-level storage volumes to tireless information storage for use with EC-2 occurrences.

Chapter # 6

Benefits of Using AWS

1. Zero CapEx:

Numerous individuals will, in general, accept that AWS or some other cloud-based arrangement is just for the wealthy. However, the fact of the matter is completely opposite. We see AWS as playing field leveler empowering new businesses to use top of the line innovations and framework needs with ZERO CapEx. New businesses avoiding utilizing Oracle as their database or some other advertisements virtual products which request high-upfront licensing cost must investigate AWS Marketplace and in high-probability, they may discover those items in an hourly estimated model with no up-front expense.

2. No-Commitment:

Regardless of whether you require a server for facilitating a little site, a Content Delivery Network (CDN) for substantial traffic sites, dependable and scalable email administration, information warehousing service, or Hadoop bunch for your Big Data needs, AWS offers everything with definitely no commitment by any means, not, in any case, a month. All server-backed services are charged on an hourly basis, so when you end/stop a server, you won't be charged from one hour from now.

3. Get Rid of Negotiations:

Surely value arrangements aren't a mastery area for some (at least me) and neither one of we likes investing our time and vitality doing that regardless of whether we have what it takes. AWS is highly focused around lessening foundation costs for its clients. They have marked down their evaluating crosswise over different administrations in excess of multiple times in the most recent couple of years. Devices like Trusted Advisor, or outsider instruments like CloudCheckr, Cloud ability, Cloudyn and so on can give you bits of knowledge to optimize cost inside your current arrangement on AWS.

4. Procurement:

Procuring another server may require a significant investment between a few hours to 8-10 days relying on whether your framework is on-premise, co-found or if you are related with a facilitating supplier. Comparative time is expected to obtain software licenses also. In any case, AWS empowers you to turn up new servers inside a couple of moments with no need to purchase separate licenses for some working frameworks and programming projects.

5. Pay Per Use:

Consider infinite space for your reinforcement and chronicled needs, the capacity to launched new servers, up-scale/downscale a server, CDN incorporation, transcoding media documents, infinite data transmission and a lot more highly adaptable administrations/highlights accessible to you while you pay depends on your real utilization as it were.

6. Security:

AWS has built a world-class, exceptionally secure foundation, both physically and over the web. Some features from the safety efforts referenced on the AWS site are:

Data centers are staffed 24×7 via prepared security monitors, and access is approved carefully on a least advantaged basis. Numerous geographic districts and

Availability Zones enable you to stay flexible even with most failure modes, including natural disasters or system failures.

Capacity to arrange worked in firewall rules from completely open to totally private or someplace in the middle of to control access to examples.

Influence Identity and Access Management (IAM) and CloudTrail to hold track of all exercises done by various clients.

Barely any different features incorporate private subnets, multi-factor authentication (MFA), Isolate GovCloud and encrypted data storage.

7. Flexibility:

Just forget about the guesswork or logical examination to distinguish your framework needs. You can use auto-scaling to build a self-overseeing foundation adjusted near the genuine need dependent on traffic/asset usage. Amazon Machine Images (AMIs) empowers you to turn up clones in numerous areas for various situations inside a couple of moments, eliminating the need to rehash the set-up steps every time.

8. Worldwide Leader:

Amazon has a worldwide presence with 10 districts, 36 accessibility zones and in excess of 50 edge areas. A few months ago, Gartner situated AWS in Leaders Quadrant of the new Magic Quadrant for Cloud Infrastructure as a Service. Gartner additionally referenced that AWS has in excess of multiple times the figure limit being used than the total aggregate of rest 14 specialist co-ops set in a similar Magic Quadrant.

9. Best-in-class PaaS Offerings:

AWS has thought of highly adaptable overseen administrations for database, reserving, data warehousing, transcoding, capacity, reinforcement, foundation the board and application management which diminishes the general time and effort spent in setting-up and dealing with the framework and along these lines impressively diminishing the go-to-market cycle for end-clients.

10. API:

APIs are accessible in different programming languages to assist you in dealing with your foundation automatically. Regardless of whether it means launching another occasion, or taking reinforcements, the sky is the limit through API. Actually, APIs are more dominant than the AWS Management Console.

If you are as yet not certain if AWS suits you need but rather might want to give it a shot, the accompanying connections may interest you:

AWS Free Tier – Most of the AWS administrations offer a free to share, to begin with.

AWS Activate Packages – If you are a beginning up, take a look at AWS Activate Packages and you may get free attributes and training to begin.

Chapter # 7

Pros and Cons:

Most enterprises know about Amazon Web Services (AWS), which has a huge number of clients. In any case, many are unconscious of exactly how broad AWS's contributions are over the broad spectrum of IT capabilities.

AWS is a distributor that conveys compute cycles from their cloud data centers at a low cost. They offer administrations that will run your whole IT condition (register, organizing, capacity, database, application administrations, and the board) from the cloud and lessen your on-premise hardware footprint.

So how did an online retailer become an IT monster? After over a time of building and running the highly scalable web application Amazon.com, the organization understood that it had built up a center competency in working massive scale innovation framework and data-centers, and set out on an a lot more extensive crucial serving another client section developers and organizations with a foundation of online administrations they can use to construct complex, adaptable applications.

In 2006, AWS formally started offering designers access to in-the-cloud framework administrations dependent on Amazon's own back-end technology stage. This launch infrastructure-as-a-service (IaaS) to another degree of accessibility and permeability inside the organization division. Before AWS launched in 2006, organizations would assume the crucial capital investment of building their very own foundation, or agreement with a seller for a fixed measure of data-center limit that they may or probably won't utilize. This decision carried the danger of paying for wasted limits or stressing that the measure of limit they forecasted was lacking to keep pace with their development.

AWS has changed the game by offering a comprehensive and demonstrated a better approach to execute and oversee the business innovation foundation. The administrations that AWS offers depend individually on back-end innovation framework, which they've gone through over 10 years incorporating with one of the most solid, adaptable and cost-effective web foundations on the planet. The AWS stage has developed quickly since the main service launch in March 2006, and it is currently the fundamental foundation for organizations around the globe, from new businesses to enterprises to government offices.

Pros:

- More than 5x the figure limit being used than the total aggregate of the other fourteen driving suppliers in the market

- 7 years in the market with a huge number of clients in more than 190 nations running each possible use case on AWS

- Groups of data centers, which it calls "districts," on the East and West Coasts of the U.S., and in Ireland, Japan, Singapore, Australia, and Brazil; it additionally has one locale committed to the U.S. central government

- Accomplished most industry-standard consistency certifications: HIPAA, SOC 1/SSAE 16/ISAE 3402 (some time ago SAS70), SOC 2, SOC 3, PCI DSS

Level 1, ISO 27001, FedRAMP, DIACAP and FISMA, ITAR, FIPS 140-2, CSA, MPAA

- Thousands of independent software sellers like SAP, Oracle, Adobe, Microsoft, Esri, and so forth have made their product accessible on AWS to clients alongside go-to-market associations with framework integrators, (for example, Capgemini, Cognizant and Wipro) that give both application advancement expertise and oversaw administrations.

Cons:

- AWS flexible load balancer (ELB) isn't prepared to deal with the same number of requests as it gets. In any case, you can buy another assistance, ELB with Auto Scaling, to check.

- AWS needs client service, designing for an all the more, in fact, a clever gathering of customers as well as those with access to technical support.

- The number of decisions can be confusing to individuals who may not communicate in the language of innovation.

In any case, is AWS for everybody? Possibly not. Here are a few considerations to remember:

The expectation to learn and adapt for a product characterized server farm is here and there soak for bigger enterprises.

Charging is incredibly confusing; NPI recommends experiencing an affiliate for an increasingly definite month to month bill

AWS does not include enterprise-grade support as a matter of course. Clients should purchase Business level help for this, which conveys up to a 10% premium on the client's general AWS spend.

Practically all enterprise clients require a custom understanding (versus the navigate understanding on the web), and crucial terms-and-conditions arrangement Have encountered prominent blackouts in late history

There's no contention that AWS has changed the manner in which organizations consume IT. In any case, that doesn't mean the way toward purchasing and dealing with AWS's contributions is simple. Like any IT buy, it's full of pitfalls particularly in case you're not perhaps the biggest client. Numerous little and fair size projects can't get the help and direction of an AWS agent.

Chapter # 8

AWS Products

Coming up next are AWS services that are accessible with AWS China (Beijing) district worked by Sinnet, and AWS China (Ningxia) area worked by NWCD. Utilization of these services requires AWS China district records and acknowledgment of the Sinnet Customer Agreement for AWS (Beijing Region) and the NWCD Customer Agreement for AWS (Ningxia Region) individually. All costs below are charge selective. For the accessible administration's list, if it's not too much trouble visit http://amazonaws.cn/about-aws/territorial item benefits/.

Find out about AWS China (Ningxia) Region Free Tier, it would be ideal if you visit https://www.amazonaws.cn/en/free/

To utilize AWS data innovation benefits outside of China, it would be ideal if you make a difference worldwide AWS Account at https://aws.amazon.com.

- Storage

- Compute

- Database

- Mobile Services

- Networking & Content Delivery

- Management Tools

- Developer Tools

- Analytics

- Messaging

- Security, Identity & Compliance

- Application Services

- Game Development

- Support

- Media Service

- Internet of Things

- Machine Learning

Amazon EC2

Amazon Elastic Compute Cloud (Amazon EC2) is a web administration that gives a resizable register limit in the cloud. It is intended to make web-scale computing simpler for developers.

Amazon EC2's basic web administration interface enables you to get and design limit with minimal friction. It gives you whole control of your computing assets and gives you a chance to run on Amazon's demonstrated registering condition. Amazon EC2 lessens the time required to acquire and boot new server cases to minutes, enabling you to rapidly scale limit, both here and there, as your computing necessities change.

Amazon Elastic Container Registry

Amazon Elastic Container Registry (ECR) is a completely overseen Docker container library that makes it simple for engineers to store, manage, and convey Docker compartment pictures. Amazon ECR is coordinated with Amazon Elastic Container Service (ECS), simplifying your improvement to the creative work process.

Amazon ECR wipes out the need to work your own container repositories or stress over scaling the hidden framework. Amazon ECR has your pictures in highly accessible and scalable engineering, enabling you to dependably convey containers for your applications.

Amazon Elastic Container Service

Amazon Elastic Container Service (ECS) is a highly scalable, amazing performance container the executive's administration that supports Docker holders and enables you to effectively run applications on an oversaw group of Amazon EC2 examples. Amazon ECS dispenses with the requirement for you to introduce, work, and scale your very own bunch the board framework.

With basic API calls, you can dispatch and stop Docker-empowered applications, question the total condition of your cluster, and access numerous recognizable features like security teams, Elastic Load Balancing, EBS volumes, and IAM jobs.

AWS Lambda

AWS Lambda gives you a chance to run code without provisioning or overseeing servers. You pay just for the figure time you expend, there is no charge when your code isn't running. With Lambda, you can run code for all intents and purposes any sort of use or backend administration, all with zero organization. Simply transfer your code and Lambda deals with everything required to run and scale your code with high accessibility. You can set up your code to naturally trigger from different AWS administrations or call it directly from any web or versatile application.

Amazon Virtual Private Cloud (VPC)

Amazon Virtual Private Cloud (Amazon VPC) gives you a chance to arrangement an intelligently isolated segment of the Amazon Web Services (AWS) Cloud where you can dispatch AWS assets in a virtual system that you characterize. You have unlimited authority over your virtual systems administration condition, including determination of your own IP address run, production of subnets, and arrangement of course tables and network gateways.

AWS Elastic Beanstalk

AWS Elastic Beanstalk is a simple to-utilize administration for sending and scaling web applications and administrations created with Java, .NET, PHP, Node.js, Python, Ruby, Go, and Docker on familiar servers, for example, Apache, Nginx, Passenger, and IIS.

You can essentially transfer your code and Elastic Beanstalk naturally handles the sending, from limit provisioning, load adjusting, auto-scaling to application health checking.

Auto Scaling

Auto Scaling enables you to scale your Amazon EC2 limit up or down consequently as indicated by conditions that you characterize. With Auto Scaling, you can guarantee that the quantity of Amazon EC2 cases you're utilizing increases consistently during request spikes to look after execution, and diminishes consequently during request breaks to limit costs. Auto Scaling is especially appropriate for applications that experience hourly, every day, or week by week inconstancy in use. Auto Scaling is empowered by Amazon CloudWatch and accessible at no extra charge past Amazon CloudWatch expenses.

Elastic Load Balancing

Elastic Load Balancing consequently distributes approaching application traffic over numerous Amazon EC2 examples. It empowers you to accomplish much more fault tolerance in your applications, consistently giving the measure of burden adjusting limit required because of approaching application traffic. Elastic Load Balancing identifies unfortunate occasions inside a pool and naturally reroutes traffic to strong cases until the undesirable examples have been restored. Clients can empower Elastic Load Balancing inside a single Availability Zone or over numerous zones for considerably progressively steady application performance.

Chapter # 9

Amazon Athena

Amazon Athena is assistance that empowers a data analyst to perform intelligent queries in the Amazon Web Services open cloud on information put away in Amazon Simple Storage Service (S3). Since Athena is a serverless query administration, an expert doesn't have to deal with any hidden register framework to utilize it.

There is additionally no reason to load S3 information into Amazon Athena or change it for examination, which makes it simpler and quicker for an expert to pick up understanding. An information examiner gets to Athena through either the AWS Management Console, an application programming interface (API) or a Java Database Connectivity driver; the person then just characterizes the outline and can begin to execute SQL questions on S3 information. An administrator can oversee access to Athena by means of AWS Identity and Access Management approaches, get to control records and Amazon S3 can arrangements. An Athena client can question encoded information with keys oversaw by AWS Key Management Service, and can also encrypt query results. Athena also empowers cross-account access to S3 cans claimed by another client.

Also, Athena utilizes oversaw data catalogs to store data and patterns identified with your pursuits on Amazon S3 information.

Supported data types and integration

Amazon Athena depends on the open-source Presto conveyed SQL query engine to empower both speedy specially appointed examination and increasingly complex requests, including window capacities, enormous joins, and aggregations. Athena can process both unstructured and organized information types, including positions like CSV, JSON, ORC, Parquet, and Avro. Athena additionally supports packed information in Snappy, Zlib, LZO and GZIP groups.

Athena coordinates with different administrations in the AWS portfolio. For instance, you can utilize it with Amazon QuickSight to envision information, or with AWS Glue to empower increasingly modern data catalog features, for example, a metadata vault, mechanized pattern and partition acknowledgment, and information pipelines dependent on Python. Athena itself utilizes Amazon S3 as a fundamental information store, which gives information excess.

Advantages

Start Querying Instantly
Serverless. No ETL.

Athena is serverless. You can rapidly query your information without having an arrangement and deal with any servers or information distribution centers. Simply point to your information in Amazon S3, characterize the mapping, and start questioning utilizing the implicit inquiry manager. Amazon Athena enables you to take advantage of every one of your information in S3 without the need to set up complex procedures to separate, change, and burden the information (ETL).

Pay per Query
Pay for information examined.

With Amazon Athena, you pay just for the queries that you run. You are charged $5 per terabyte filtered by your queries. You can spare from 30% to 90% on your per-question costs and show signs of improvement execution by packing, dividing, and changing over your information into columnar arrangements. Athena questions information directly in Amazon S3. There are no extra storage charges beyond S3.

Open. Powerful. Standard
Based on Presto. Runs standard SQL.

Amazon Athena utilizes Presto with ANSI SQL backing and works with a variety of standard information groups, including CSV, JSON, ORC, Avro, and Parquet. Athena is perfect for speedy, specially appointed questioning however it can also deal with complex examination, including enormous joins, window capacities, and clusters. Amazon Athena is highly accessible and executes questions utilizing figure assets over different offices and various gadgets in every office. Amazon Athena utilizes Amazon S3 as its hidden data store, making your information exceptionally accessible and strong.

Quick. Really Fast.

Intelligent execution in any event, for large datasets

With Amazon Athena, you don't need to stress over having enough register assets to get quick, intelligent question execution. Amazon Athena naturally executes queries in parallel, so most outcomes return inside seconds.

Secure:

With the assistance of IAM strategies and AWS Identity, Athena gives you unlimited oversight over the informational collection. As the information is put away in S3 cans, IAM arrangements can assist you with overseeing control to clients.

Highly available:

With the confirmation of AWS, Athena is profoundly accessible and the client can execute queries round the clock. As AWS is 99.999% accessible, so is Athena.

Integration:

The best component of Athena is that it tends to be coordinated with AWS Glue. AWS Glue will assist the client in creating a better-unified data repository. This encourages you to make better forming of information, better tables, sees, and so on.

Chapter # 10

S3 data Query with SQL

In this post, we'll perceive how we can set up a table in Athena utilizing an example informational index put away in S3 as a .csv record. However, for this, we first need that example CSV record. You can download it here.

When you have the record downloaded, make another container in AWS S3. I propose making another can with the goal that you can utilize that bucket only for evaluating Athena. Yet, you can utilize any current bucket also.

When you have the record downloaded, make another bucket in AWS S3. I recommend making another bucket with the goal that you can utilize that bucket exclusively for evaluating Athena. However, you can utilize any current can also.

Thus, since you have the record in S3, open up Amazon Athena. You'll get a choice to make a table on the Athena landing page. Mine looks something like the screen capture below, in light of the fact that I as of now have a couple of tables. As should be obvious from the screen capture, you have numerous alternatives to make a table. For this post, we'll stay with the basics and select the "Make table from S3 pail information" option. So, since you have the document in S3, open up Amazon Athena. You'll get a choice to make a table on the Athena landing page. Mine looks something like the screen capture below, on the grounds that I as of now have a couple of tables. As should be obvious from the screen capture, you have numerous alternatives to make a table. For this post, we'll stay with the basics and select the "Make the table from S3 container information" choice.

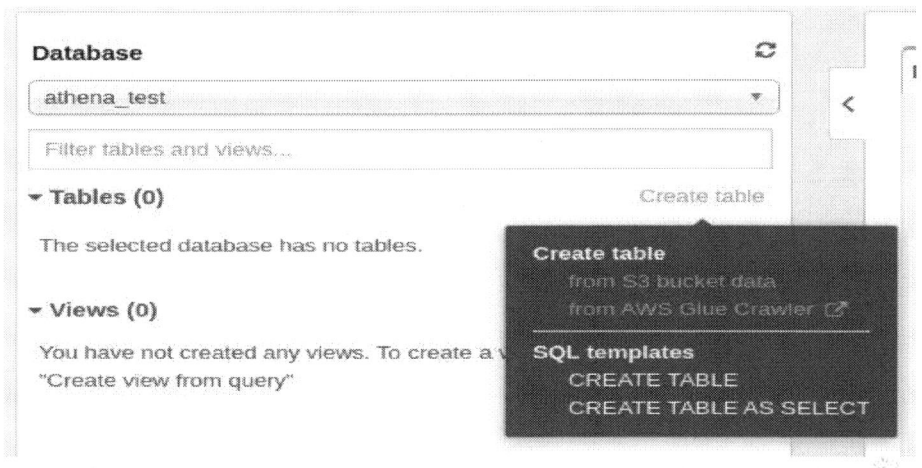

When you select that alternative, you'll be diverted to a four-step procedure of making a table. How about we take a look at every one of these means quickly.

Stage 1: Name and Location

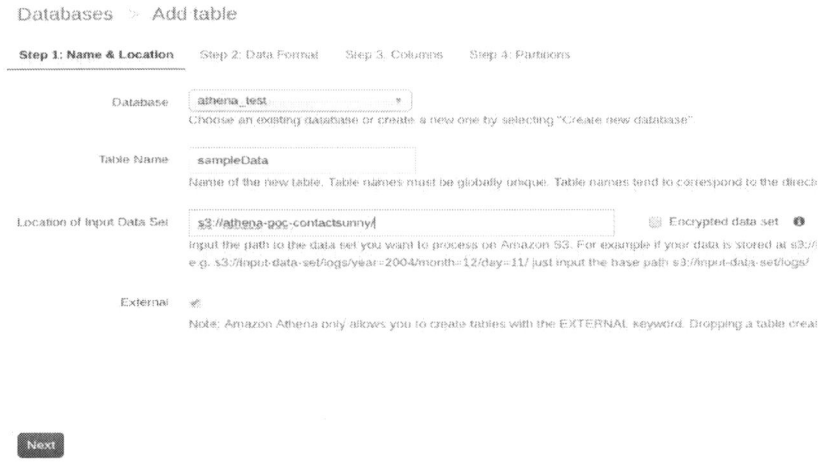

As should be obvious from the screen above, in this progression, we characterize the database, the table name, and the S3 organizer from where the information for this table will be sourced. In the event that you as of now have a database, you can choose it starting from the drop, similar to what I've done. If not, you have the alternative of making a database directly from this screen.

Next, give a name to the table. For this model, I've named the table sample data, just to keep it the same as the CSV document I'm utilizing.

Next, you need to give the way of the organizer in S3 where you have the record put away. Note that you can't give the document way, you can just give the organizer way. So every one of the documents in that envelope with the coordinating record configuration will be utilized as the information source. Since we just have one document, our information will be constrained to that. We'll ignore the encryption options in this post.

How about we additionally note here that Athena doesn't duplicate over any information from these source documents to another area, memory or storage. Each question is run against the first data set.

Stage 2: Data Format

This is a truly straight forward advance. You simply select the document organization of your information source. Since we're utilizing a CSV record, we'll select CSV as the information design.

Databases > Add table

Step 1: Name & Location   **Step 2: Data Format**   Step 3: Columns   Step 4: Partitions

Data Format
- ⚪ Apache Web Logs
- 🔘 CSV
- ⚪ TSV
- ⚪ Text File with Custom Delimiters
- ⚪ JSON
- ⚪ Parquet
- ⚪ ORC

Back   Next

Stage 3: Columns

Databases > Add table

Step 1: Name & Location   Step 2: Data Format   **Step 3: Columns**   Step 4: Partitions

Column Name   _id
Column name must be single words that start with a letter or a digit.

Column type   string ▾
Type for this column. Certain advanced types (namely, structs) are not exposed in this interface.

Column Name   string1
Column name must be single words that start with a letter or a digit.

Column type   string ▾
Type for this column. Certain advanced types (namely, structs) are not exposed in this interface.

Column Name   string2
Column name must be single words that start with a letter or a digit.

Column type   string ▾
Type for this column. Certain advanced types (namely, structs) are not exposed in this interface.

Column Name   double1
Column name must be single words that start with a letter or a digit.

Column type   double ▾
Type for this column. Certain advanced types (namely, structs) are not exposed in this interface.

In this third step, we characterize the "columns" or the fields in each report/record in our data set. This is required so Athena knows the construction of the information we're working with. Any field or section which isn't defined here, or has a grammatical error in the name, i.e., misconfigured, will be replaced and ignored with void values. So ensure you design the columns appropriately.

In the event that your informational collection has such a large number of columns, and it gets repetitive to design every one of them independently, you can include sections in mass also. You'll discover the choice for that at the base of the page. For instance, the mass arrangement for our model resembles this:

_id string, string1 string, string2 string, double1 double, double2 double

As should be obvious, the configuration is really basic. You indicate the name of the segment, followed by a space, trailed by the kind of information in that section. Section definitions are delimited utilizing a comma.

Stage 4: Partitions

This progression is somewhat advanced, which manages segments. Since our information is entirely little, and furthermore in light of the fact that it is somewhat out of the extent of this specific post, we'll skirt this progression until further notice. So overlook this progression, and confirm the remainder of the design.

Your Athena query arrangement is presently finished. You'll be taken to the query page. Here, you'll get the CREATE TABLE inquiry with the question used to make the table we simply arranged. You don't need to run this query, as the table is as of now made and is recorded in the left sheet. This query is shown here just for your reference. Possibly you can make this query manually next time as opposed to experiencing three to four stages in the console.

```
New query 1        New query 2  +
    1  CREATE EXTERNAL TABLE IF NOT EXISTS athena_test.sampleData (
    2      `_id` string,
    3      `string1` string,
    4      `string2` string,
    5      `double1` double,
    6      `double2` double
    7  )
    8  ROW FORMAT SERDE 'org.apache.hadoop.hive.serde2.lazy.LazySimpleSerDe'
    9  WITH SERDEPROPERTIES (
   10     'serialization.format' = ',',
   11     'field.delim' = ','
   12  ) LOCATION 's3://athena-poc-contactsunny/'
   13  TBLPROPERTIES ('has_encrypted_data'='false');
```

Run query   Save as   Create ▾   (Run time: 0.31 seconds, Data scanned: 0 KB)

Use Ctrl + Enter to run query, Ctrl + Space to autocomplete

What's remaining to this query is legitimate. To test this out, we'll run this simple SQL query:

Select * from sampledata limit 10;

After running this question, your result should be like the accompanying screen capture.

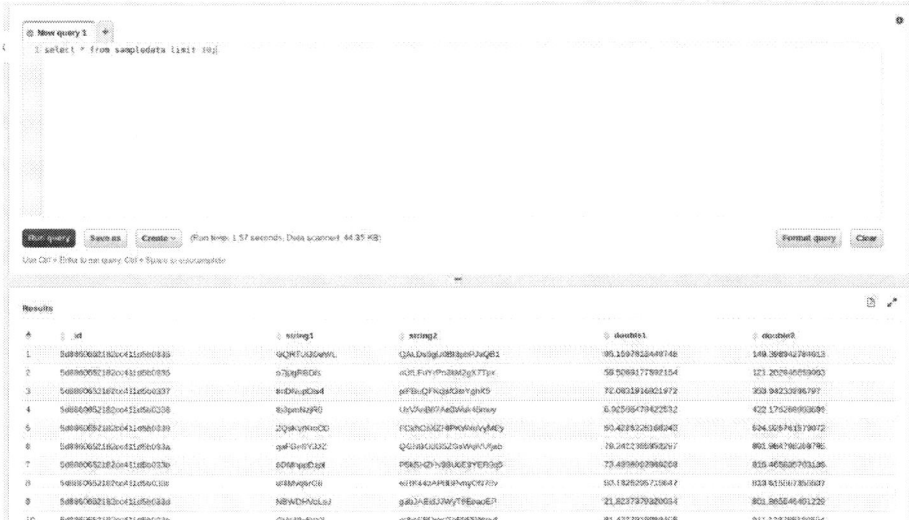

Chapter # 11

What Is Amazon EC2?

Amazon Elastic Compute Cloud (Amazon EC2) gives an adaptable processing limit in the Amazon Web Services (AWS) cloud. Utilizing Amazon EC2 wipes out your need to put resources into equipment in advance, so you can create and deploy applications quicker. You can utilize Amazon EC2 to launch the same number of or as not many virtual servers as you need, design security and organizing, and manage storage. Amazon EC2 empowers you to scale up or down to deal with changes in necessities or spikes in popularity, decreasing your need to forecast traffic.

Features of Amazon EC2

Amazon EC2 gives the accompanying features:

- Virtual computing conditions, known as examples

- Preconfigured layouts for your cases, known as Amazon Machine Images (AMIs), that bundle the bits your requirement for your server (counting the working framework and extra software)

- Various arrangements of CPU, memory, storage, and systems administration limit with regards to your occurrences, known as for example types

- Secure login data for your examples utilizing key sets (AWS stores the general population key, and you store the private key in a protected spot)

- Storage volumes for brief information that is erased when you stop or end your occurrence, known as case store volumes

- Persistent storage volumes for your information utilizing Amazon Elastic Block Store (Amazon EBS), known as Amazon EBS volumes

- Multiple physical areas for your assets, for example, cases and Amazon EBS volumes, known as Regions and Availability Zones

- A firewall that empowers you to indicate the protocols, ports, and source IP goes that can arrive at your cases utilizing security teams

- Static IPv4 addresses for dynamic distributed computing, known as Elastic IP addresses

- Metadata, known as labels, that you can make and relegate to your Amazon EC2 assets

- Virtual systems you can make that are logically isolated from the remainder of the AWS cloud and that you can alternatively interface with your own system, known as virtual private clouds (VPCs)

Step by step instructions to Get Started with Amazon EC2

To start with, you have to get set up to utilize Amazon EC2. After you are set up, you are prepared to finish the Getting Started instructional exercise for Amazon EC2. At whatever point you need more data about an Amazon EC2 include, you can peruse the technical documentation.

Get Up and Running

- Setting Up with Amazon EC2

- Getting Started with Amazon EC2 Linux Instances

Basics

- Tags

- Instances and AMIs

- Instance Types

- Regions and Availability Zones

Networking and Security

- Security Groups

- Amazon EC2 Key Pairs

- Amazon EC2 and Amazon VPC

- Elastic IP Addresses

Storage

- Instance Store

- Amazon EBS

Working with Linux Instances

- AWS Systems Manager Run Command in the AWS Systems Manager User Guide

- Tutorial: Install a LAMP Web Server on Amazon Linux 2

- Tutorial: Configure SSL/TLS on Amazon Linux 2

- Getting Started with AWS: Hosting a Web App for Linux

Accessing Amazon EC2

Amazon EC2 gives a web-based UI, the Amazon EC2 comfort. In the event that you've pursued an AWS account, you can get to the Amazon EC2 reassure by marking into the AWS Management Console and choosing EC2 from the comfort home page.

If you want to utilize a direction line interface, you have the accompanying options:

AWS Command Line Interface (CLI)

Provides commands to a broad set of AWS items, and is upheld on Windows, Mac, and Linux. To begin, see the AWS Command Line Interface User Guide. For more data about the directions for Amazon EC2, see ec2 in the AWS CLI Command Reference.

AWS Tools for Windows PowerShell

Provides commands to a broad set of AWS items for the individuals who content in the PowerShell condition. To begin, see the AWS Tools for Windows PowerShell User Guide. For more data about the cmdlets for Amazon EC2, see the AWS Tools for PowerShell Cmdlet Reference.

Pricing for Amazon EC2

At the point when you sign up for AWS, you can begin with Amazon EC2 with the expectation of complimentary utilizing the AWS Free Tier.

Amazon EC2 gives the accompanying buying alternatives to occasions:

On-Demand Instances

Pay for the occurrences that you use continuously, with no long haul duties or upfront installments.

Savings Plans

You can diminish your Amazon EC2 costs by making a guarantee to a steady measure of use, in USD every hour, for a term of 1 or 3 years.

Reserved Instances

You can lessen your Amazon EC2 costs by making a promise to a particular example design, including occurrence type and Region, for a term of 1 or 3 years.

Chapter # 12

Amazon CloudSearch

Amazon CloudSearch is a managed administration in the AWS Cloud that makes it simple and practical to set up, oversee, and scale a search solution for your site or application.

Amazon CloudSearch supports 34 languages and prominent search features, for example, featuring, autocomplete, and geospatial search.

Benefits

With Amazon CloudSearch, you can rapidly add rich search capacities to your site or application. You don't have to turn into a search master or stress over equipment provisioning, arrangement, and support. With a couple of clicks in the AWS Management Console, you can make a search domain and transfer the information that you need to make accessible, and Amazon CloudSearch will automatically set up the necessary assets and convey a highly tuned search list.

You can without much of a stretch change your search parameters, calibrate search pertinence, and apply new settings whenever. As your volume of information and traffic fluctuates, Amazon CloudSearch flawlessly scales to address your issues.

Simple

You can arrange and deal with an Amazon CloudSearch area through the AWS Management Console, AWS CLI, and AWS SDKs. Basically, point to an example of your information and Amazon CloudSearch will consequently prescribe how to arrange your space's ordering choices. You can easily delete or add list fields and customize search choices, for example, faceting and featuring. Design changes don't expect you to re-upload your information.

Scalable

Amazon CloudSearch offers ground-breaking auto-scaling for all search areas. As your information or question volume changes, Amazon CloudSearch can scale your search space's assets up or down as required. You can control scaling if you realize that you need a greater limit with regards to mass transfers or are anticipating a surge in search traffic.

Reliable

Amazon CloudSearch gives programmed checking and recuperation to your search spaces. When Multi-AZ is empowered, Amazon CloudSearch arrangements and keeps up assets for search area in two Availability Zones to guarantee high accessibility. Updates are consequently applied to the inquiry occasions in both Availability Zones. Search traffic is dispersed crosswise over both Availability Zones and the cases in either zone are fit for dealing with the full burden in case of a failure.

High Performance

Amazon CloudSearch guarantees low latency and high throughput performance, even everywhere scale through programmed sharing and flat and vertical auto-scaling.

Fully Managed

Amazon CloudSearch is a completely overseen custom search administration. Equipment and programming provisioning, arrangement and design, programming fixing, information partitioning, node checking, scaling, and information durability are taken care of for you.

Rich Search Features

Amazon CloudSearch supports powerful search highlights, for example,

- Autocomplete suggestions

- Free content, Boolean, and Faceted search

- Field weighting

- Customizable significance positioning and search time rank articulations

- Highlighting

- Support for 34 languages

- Geospatial search

Cost-Effective

Amazon CloudSearch is intended to be cost-effective. You pay low hourly rates, and just for the assets, you use. Amazon CloudSearch offers a low cost of ownership for your search applications compared with the working search domain all alone. For point by point evaluating data, see Pricing.

Secure

Amazon CloudSearch utilizes strong cryptographic techniques to verify clients and anticipate unapproved access to your areas. Amazon CloudSearch supports HTTPS and coordinates with Identity and Access Management (IAM) to control access to the CloudSearch arrangement administration and every space's archive, search, and propose administrations.

New/Enhanced Search Features

Here are our top picks:

Proximity searching: A NEAR administrator has been included

Term boosting: This is helpful for fine-grain pertinence tuning.

Better range searching: This can be utilized with all field types (numbers, dates...)

Native Geo support: For instance, to arrange indexed lists in good ways from a particular area. This is a significant online business work.

Various/Optional Query Parsers: CloudSearch now supports basic, organized, Lucene, and dismax parsers, giving adaptability, as far as how queries are prepared, and how relevancy is determined. These generally low-level capacities don't get business people energized. In any case, they are significant instruments with which specialized people make and tune incredible search frameworks.

Size/Scale Options: CloudSearch now gives better power over how your search application will scale, as the load is applied.

Language Support

CloudSearch now offers help for 32 languages, as recorded below. Backing incorporates language-explicit content examination, and both algorithmic and word reference support for stemming. The language can be characterized at a field level, which can be valuable in multi-lingual conditions.

Chapter # 13

Amazon Elasticsearch Service

Amazon Elasticsearch Service is a completely managed administration that makes it simple for you to send, secure, and work Elasticsearch at scale with zero downtime. The administration offers open-source Elasticsearch APIs, oversaw Kibana, and mixes with Logstash and different AWS Services, empowering you to safely ingest information from any source and search, break down, and imagine it progressively. Amazon Elasticsearch Service gives you a chance to pay just for what you use, there are no upfront expenses or utilization necessities. With Amazon Elasticsearch Service, you get the ELK stack you need, without the operational overhead.

Advantages

Simple TO DEPLOY AND MANAGE

With Amazon Elasticsearch Service you can send a generation prepared Elasticsearch group in minutes. Amazon Elasticsearch Service simplifies management projects, for example, equipment provisioning, programming introducing and fixing, failure recovery, reinforcements, and observing, allowing you to reduce operational overhead and assemble inventive applications.

Incorporated WITH OPEN-SOURCE TOOLS and AWS SERVICES

Amazon Elasticsearch Service offers access to open-source Elasticsearch APIs, oversaw Kibana, and combination with Logstash, so you can keep on utilizing your current code and information ingestion and perception tool. The administration also offers worked in integrations with different AWS administrations, for example, Amazon Kinesis Data Warehouse, AWS IoT, and Amazon CloudWatch Logs for information ingestion; AWS CloudTrail for inspecting; Amazon VPC, AWS KMS, Amazon Cognito, and AWS IAM for security.

Effectively SCALABLE

Amazon Elasticsearch Service gives you a chance to scale effectively and quickly as your business requirement changes. You can scale your group up or down by means of a single API call or a couple of snaps.

You can also design your bunch to meet your presentation necessities by choosing from a scope of example types and capacity alternatives including SSD-fueled EBS volumes.

SECURE AND COMPLIANT

Utilizing Amazon Elasticsearch Service, you can accomplish organize isolation with Amazon VPC, encode information very still and in-travel utilizing keys you make and control through AWS KMS, and oversee validation and access control with Amazon Cognito and AWS IAM strategies. Amazon Elasticsearch Service is additionally HIPAA qualified, and agreeable with PCI DSS and ISO guidelines to assist you with meeting industry-explicit or administrative necessities.

HIGHLY AVAILABLE

Amazon Elasticsearch Service is intended to be exceptionally accessible utilizing multi-AZ organizations, which duplicates information between various Availability Zones in a similar locale. The administration likewise screens the strength of bunches and naturally replaces failed cases.

COST-EFFECTIVE

With Amazon Elasticsearch Service, you pay just for what you use. There is no upfront expense or utilization necessity. With worked in encryption and VPC support, 24x7 checking, and AWS support, you needn't bother with a group of Elasticsearch specialists to scale, secure, and screen your foundation, bringing about lower all out the cost of tasks.

Use cases

LOG ANALYTICS

Examine unstructured and semi-structured logs created by sites, cell phones, servers, and sensors and so on. For operational knowledge, application checking, underlying driver investigation, and the sky is the limit from there. Catch, pre-procedure, and burden log information into Amazon Elasticsearch Service utilizing Amazon Kinesis Firehouse, Logstash, or Amazon CloudWatch Logs, and hence, search, investigate, and envision the information utilizing Kibana and the Elasticsearch question DSL to increase significant experiences about your clients and applications.

Adobe utilizes Amazon Elasticsearch Service to cost-effectively examine and envision the huge measure of log information for its Developer Platform, which at the top gets over 200K API calls every second. With Amazon Elasticsearch Service, Adobe can without much of a stretch see traffic examples and blunder rates and rapidly recognize and investigate any potential issues - all with diminished operational overhead.

REAL-TIME APPLICATION MONITORING

Catch action logs over your client-facing applications and sites for ongoing application checking and issue goals. Push these logs to your Amazon Elasticsearch Service area utilizing Logstash. Elasticsearch files the information, makes it accessible for investigation continuously, and enables you to imagine the information utilizing the inherent Kibana module.

Expedia utilizes Amazon Elasticsearch Service for application observing and main driver investigation and value advancement. Amazon Elasticsearch empowers Expedia to monitor huge volumes of Docker logs cost-successfully, recognize and investigate issues continuously, scale effectively to suit extra log sources, and offload the operational overhead.

SECURITY ANALYTICS

Empowers security professionals to incorporate and investigate occasions from over the whole association to upgrade occurrence reaction and monitor threats over the entirety of their applications and frameworks progressively. Amazon Elasticsearch Service enables you to record the information when it is ingested enabling you to break down and imagine information from different sources in a flash and discover and counteract threats quicker.

Chapter # 14

Cluster Elasticsearch execution and resizing

Resize Your Cluster

Elasticsearch scales to whatever limit you need and with the same number of hubs as the accessible assets can support. In the event that you need more accessible assets, include some limit first.

1. To resize a group:

2. Log into the Cloud UI.

3. Click on a group name from the Clusters board and snap Manage.

4. Click Edit setup.

5. Change the cluster configuration

Fault tolerance

If you made use of just a single accessibility zone, it doesn't fault-tolerant. On a generation framework, empower high accessibility by changing your group to use at any rate two accessibility zones, three for crucial organizations.

Node Capacity

Node limit should be adequate to continue your pursuit of outstanding tasks at hand, regardless of whether you lose an accessibility zone. Right now, half of the memory is allotted to the JVM load. For instance, on a group with 32 GB RAM, 16 GB are allocated to the store. Up to 64 GB RAM and 1 TB storage for each node are supported.

Node Count

Including more nodes gives you a chance to scale out on a level plane by adding all the more preparing ability to your bunch.

2. Click Save changes.

Example: From Very Small to Very Large

The main group we provisioned was essential: It utilized just a single accessibility area and a single node. In this model, you change a similar cluster to utilize high accessibility and to include a limit.

To scale your group from extremely little to exceptionally huge:

3. Log into the Cloud UI.

4. Click on a group name from the Clusters board and snap Manage.

5. Click Edit design.

6. Under Fault tolerance, select 3 zones — for strategic conditions.

7. Under the Node limit, select 64 GB memory/2 TB stockpiling.

8. Click Save changes.

There is no personal time while including high accessibility or expanding cluster limit. Your group keeps on taking care of client demands as the setup change gets applied.

Chapter # 15

Amazon EMR

Amazon EMR is the business driving cloud-local big data platform, enabling groups to process tremendous measures of information rapidly, and cost-successfully at scale. Utilizing open-source devices, for example, Apache Spark, Apache Hive, Apache HBase, Apache Flink, and Presto, combined with the dynamic scalability of Amazon EC2 and adaptable storage of Amazon S3, EMR gives systematic groups the motors and flexibility to run Petabyte-scale investigation for a small amount of the expense of customary on-premise clusters. Engineers and examiners can utilize Jupyter-based EMR Notebooks for iterative improvement, cooperation, and access to information put away crosswise over AWS information items, for example, Amazon S3, Amazon DynamoDB, and Amazon Redshift to diminish time to understanding and rapidly operationalize analytics.

Clients across numerous industry verticals use EMR to safely and dependably handle wide arrangements of enormous information use cases, including AI, information changes (ETL), monetary and logical reenactment, bioinformatics, log investigation, and deep learning. EMR gives groups the adaptability to run use cases on single-purpose short-lived clusters that consequently scale to satisfy a need, or on long-running profoundly accessible groups utilizing the new multi-ace sending mode.

Advantages

Easy TO USE

EMR launches groups in minutes. You don't have to stress over node provisioning, framework arrangement, Hadoop setup, or bunch tuning. EMR deals with these projects so you can concentrate on examination. Experts, information architects, and information researchers can dispatch a serverless Jupyter scratchpad in seconds utilizing EMR Notebooks, enabling people and groups to work together and intelligently investigate, process and envision information in a simple to utilize note pad design.

LOW COST

EMR pricing is basic and unsurprising: You pay for each case rate for consistently utilized, with a one-minute least charge. You can launch a 10-hub EMR group with applications, for example, Apache Spark, and Apache Hive, for as meager as $0.15 every hour. Since EMR has local help for Amazon EC2 Spot and Reserved Instances, you can also save 50-80% on the expense of the fundamental examples.

ELASTIC

With EMR, you can arrange one, hundreds, or thousands of register examples to process information at any scale. The number of occurrences can be expanded or diminished physically or consequently utilizing Auto Scaling (which oversees bunch sizes dependent on usage), and you pay for what you use. In contrast to the unbending framework of on-premise groups, EMR decouples compute and persistent storage, enabling you to scale each autonomously.

RELIABLE

Invest less energy tuning and observing your bunch. EMR is tuned for the cloud and continually monitors your group, retrying failed tasks and automatically replacing ineffectively performing examples. EMR gives the most recent stable open-source programming releases, so you don't need to oversee updates and bug fixes, leading fewer issues and less exertion to keep up nature. With different ace hubs, groups are exceptionally accessible and consequently failover in case of a node failure.

SECURE

EMR consequently arranges EC2 firewall settings controlling system access to occurrences and launches clusters in an Amazon Virtual Private Cloud (VPC), a logically isolated system you characterize. For objects put away in S3, server-side encryption or customer side encryption can be utilized with EMRFS (an article store for Hadoop on S3), utilizing the AWS Key Management Service or your very own client oversaw keys. EMR makes it simple to empower other encryption alternatives, as in-travel and very still encryption, and strong authentication with Kerberos.

FLEXIBLE

You have full control over your cluster. You have root access to each occasion, you can undoubtedly introduce extra applications, and redo each group with bootstrap activities. You can likewise dispatch EMR clusters with custom Amazon Linux AMIs, and reconfigure running groups on the fly without the need to re-dispatch the group.

Use cases

MACHINE LEARNING

Utilize EMR's worked in AI instruments, including Apache Spark MLlib, TensorFlow, and Apache MXNet for scalable AI calculations, and utilize Custom AMI's and Bootstrap Actions to effortlessly include your favored libraries and tools to make your own predictive investigation toolset.

REAL-TIME STREAMING

Break down occasions from Apache Kafka, Amazon Kinesis, or other gushing information sources continuously with Apache Spark Streaming and EMR to make long-running, highly accessible, and fault-tolerant streaming data pipelines. Endure changed informational collections to Amazon S3 or HDFS, and bits of knowledge to Amazon Elasticsearch.

INTERACTIVE ANALYTICS

EMR Notebooks give a managed analytic condition dependent on open-source Jupyter that permits data researchers, experts, and designers to plan and picture information, team up with peers, fabricate applications, and perform intelligent examination.

Chapter # 16

Framework Hadoop

Apache Hadoop is one of the most generally utilized open-source tools for understanding Big Data. In the present carefully determined world, each association needs to understand information on a progressing basis. Hadoop is a whole biological system of Big Data devices and advancements, which is progressively being sent for putting away and parsing of Big Data.

Definition of Apache Hadoop

It is an open-source information stage or structure created in Java, devoted to store and break down enormous arrangements of unstructured data.

With the information exploding from advanced media, the world is getting overwhelmed with the forefront of Big Data advances. In any case, Apache Hadoop was the first which mirrored this flood of advancement. Give us a chance to discover what Hadoop programming is and its biological system. In this blog, we will find out about the whole Hadoop biological system that incorporates Hadoop applications, Hadoop Common, and Hadoop structure.

Features of Apache Hadoop:

- Allows different simultaneous projects to run from single to a huge number of servers immediately

- Consists of a distributed file framework that permits moving information and documents in split seconds between various nodes

- Able to process productively regardless of whether a node fails

Hadoop Components	Tasks Performed
Common	Carries libraries and utilities used by other modules
HDFS	Allows storing huge data across multiple machines
YARN	Responsible for splitting the functionalities and scheduling the jobs
MapReduce	Processes each task into two sequential steps, i.e., the map task and the reduce task

How did Apache Hadoop evolve?

Inspired by Google's MapReduce, which parts an application into little portions to run on various hubs, researchers Doug Cutting and Mike Cafarella made a stage called Hadoop 1.0 and propelled it in the year 2006 to help the distribution of Nutch web index.

Apache Hadoop was made accessible for people in general in November 2012 by Apache Software Foundation. Named after a yellow soft toy elephant of Doug Cutting's child, this innovation has been persistently revised since its launch.

As a feature of its modification, Apache Software Foundation propelled its second reconsidered variant Hadoop 2.3.0 on February 20, 2014, with some significant changes in the engineering.

What comprises the Hadoop data architecture/ecosystem?

The design can be separated into two branches, i.e., Hadoop center segments and complementary/other components.

Core Hadoop Components

There are four essential or center parts:

Hadoop Common: It is a lot of normal utilities and libraries which handle other Hadoop modules. It ensures that the equipment failures are managed by the Hadoop group consequently.

HDFS: It is a Hadoop Distributed File System that stores information as little memory squares and circulates them over the group. Each data is replicated on numerous occasions to guarantee information availability.

Hadoop YARN: It designates assets which thus enable various clients to execute different applications without worrying over the expanded remaining tasks at hand.

Hadoop MapReduce: It executes errands in a parallel design by distributing the information as little blocks.

Ambari: Ambari is a web-based interface for managing, designing, and testing Big Data bunches to help its parts, for example, HDFS, MapReduce, Hive, HCatalog, HBase, ZooKeeper, Oozie, Pig, and Sqoop. It gives comfort to observing the health of the bunches just as permits surveying the exhibition of specific parts, for example, MapReduce, Pig, Hive, and so on in an easy to understand way.

Cassandra: It is an open-source, scalable distributed database framework dependent on NoSQL committed to deal with big measures of information over different ware servers, at last adding to high accessibility without a single failure.

Flume: Flume is a distributed and solid apparatus for adequately gathering, collecting, and moving the greater part of streaming information into HDFS.

HBase: HBase is a non-social appropriated database running on the Big Data Hadoop group that stores a lot of organized information. It goes about as a contribution to the MapReduce employments.

HCatalog: It is a layer of table and capacity the board which enables engineers to access and share information.

Hive: Hive is an information distribution center framework that permits to summarize, query, and analyze information with the assistance of query language like SQL.

Oozie: Oozie is a server-based framework that timetables and deals with the Hadoop occupations.

Pig: A dedicated significant level stage, Pig is answerable for controlling information put away in HDFS with the assistance of a compiler for MapReduce and a language called Pig Latin. It enables experts to separate, change, and burden (ETL) the information without writing codes for MapReduce.

Solr: A highly scalable search tool, Solr empowers ordering, focal design, failovers, and recovery.

Flash: An open-source quick motor liable for Hadoop spilling and supporting SQL, AI and preparing diagrams.

Sqoop: It is an instrument to move tremendous measures of information among Hadoop and organized databases.

ZooKeeper: An open-source application, ZooKeeper designs and synchronizes the conveyed frameworks.

Chapter # 17

Amazon Kinesis

You can utilize Amazon Kinesis Data Streams to gather and process enormous floods of information records progressively. You can make information handling applications, known as Kinesis Data Streams applications. A normal Kinesis Data Streams application reads information from an information stream as information records. These applications can utilize the Kinesis Client Library, and they can run on Amazon EC2 occurrences. You can send the prepared records to dashboards, use them to produce alerts, progressively change evaluating and publicizing systems, or send information to an assortment of different AWS administrations. For data about Kinesis Data Streams features and evaluating, see Amazon Kinesis Data Streams.

Kinesis Data Streams is a piece of the Kinesis streaming data platform, alongside Kinesis Data Firehose, Kinesis Video Streams, and Kinesis Data Analytics.

What Can I Do with Kinesis Data Streams?

You can utilize Kinesis Data Streams for fast and constant information admission and total. The sort of information utilized can incorporate IT foundation log information, application logs, online networking, advertise information feeds, and web clickstream information. Since the reaction time for the information admission and handling is progressive, the preparing is regularly lightweight.

The following are typical scenarios for using Kinesis Data Streams:

Accelerated log and data feed intake and processing

You can have makers push information directly into a stream. For instance, push framework and application logs and they are accessible for handling in a flash. This keeps the log information from being lost if the front end or application server comes up short. Kinesis Data Streams gives quickened information feed consumption since you don't group the information on the servers before you submit it for intake.

Real-time metrics and reporting

You can utilize information gathered into Kinesis Data Streams for basic information investigation and reporting continuously. For instance, your information handling application can work on the measurements and detailing for framework and application logs as the information is streaming in, as opposed to standing by to get clusters of information.

Real-time data analytics

This combines the intensity of parallel handling with the estimation of real-time information. For instance, process site clickstreams progressively, and later look at the site ease of use commitment utilizing various distinctive Kinesis Data Streams applications running in parallel.

Complex stream processing

You can make Directed Acyclic Graphs (DAGs) of Kinesis Data Streams applications and information streams. This ordinarily includes putting information from various Kinesis Data Streams applications into another stream for stream preparing by an alternate Kinesis Data Streams application.

Advantages of Using Kinesis Data Streams

Despite the fact that you can utilize Kinesis Data Streams to understand a variety of streaming information issues, typical use is the constant collection of information followed by storing the total information into a data warehouse or map-reduce cluster.

Information is placed into Kinesis information streams, which guarantees elasticity and durability. The delay between the time a record is placed into the stream and the time it tends to be recovered (put-to-get delay) is normally under 1 second. As it were, a Kinesis Data Streams application can begin expending the information from the stream very quickly after the information is included. The managed administration part of Kinesis Data Streams relieves you of the operational weight of making and running an information admission pipeline. You can make spilling map-decrease type applications. The flexibility of Kinesis Data Streams enables you to scale the stream up or down, with the goal that you never lose information records they expire. Numerous Kinesis Data Streams applications can consume information from a stream, with the goal that different activities, such as filing and preparing, can happen simultaneously and autonomously. For instance, two applications can read information from a similar stream. The principal application calculates running totals and updates an Amazon DynamoDB table and the second application packs and archives information to an information store like Amazon Simple Storage Service (Amazon S3). The DynamoDB table with running totals is then read by a dashboard for expert reports.

The Kinesis Client Library enables fault-tolerant utilization of information from streams and gives scaling backing to Kinesis Data Streams applications.

Chapter # 18

What is Streaming Data?

Streaming Data will be information that is produced constantly by a great many information sources, which regularly send in the data records all the while, and in little sizes (request of Kilobytes). Streaming information incorporates a wide assortment of information, for example, log records created by clients utilizing your mobile or web applications, eCommerce purchases, in-game player movement, data from interpersonal organizations, financial trading floors, or geospatial administrations, and telemetry from associated gadgets or instrumentation in data centers.

This information should be prepared consecutively and incrementally on a record-by-record premise or over sliding time windows, and utilized for a wide assortment of examination including connections, aggregations, separating, and inspecting. Data got from such investigation gives organizations perceivability into numerous parts of their business and client movement, for example, administration use (for metering/billing), server action, site clicks, and geo-area of gadgets, individuals, and physical products and enables them to react quickly to rising circumstances. For instance, organizations can follow changes in open feeling on their brands and items by persistently breaking down internet-based lifestreams, and react in a convenient style as the need emerges.

Advantages of Streaming Data

Streaming Data handling is useful in many situations where new, powerful information is created consistently. It applies to the vast majority of the business sections and huge information use cases. Organizations by and large start with basic applications, for example, gathering framework logs and simple preparing like moving min-max calculations. At that point, these applications develop to increasingly complex close ongoing preparing. At first, applications may process information streams to deliver simple reports, and perform basic activities accordingly, for example, emitting alarms when key measures surpass certain edges. Eventually, those applications perform progressively complex types of information examination, such as applying AI calculations and concentrate further bits of knowledge from the information. After some time, complex, stream and occasion handling calculations, such as rotting time windows to locate the latest prominent motion pictures, are applied, further enhancing the bits of knowledge.

Streaming Data Examples

- Sensors in transportation vehicles, mechanical hardware, and farm machinery send information to a streaming application. The application screens performance recognizes any potential defects ahead of time and puts in an extra part request consequently anticipating hardware downtime.

- A financial institution tracks changes in the securities exchange progressively, registers value-at-risk, and naturally rebalances portfolios dependent on stock value developments.

- A value-at-risk site tracks a subset of information from shoppers' cell phones and makes ongoing property proposals of properties to visit dependent on their geo-area.

- A solar power organization needs to keep up control throughput for its clients, or pay punishments. It executed a streaming information application that screens of all of the boards in the field, and schedules service continuously, in this manner limiting the times of low throughput from each board and the related penalty payouts.

- A media distributor streams billions of clickstream records from its online properties, totals and advances the information with statistic data about clients, and advances content arrangement on its webpage, conveying the significance and better understanding to its audience.

A web-based gaming organization gathers streaming information about player-game cooperation's and feeds the information into its gaming stage. It at that point breaks down the information progressively, offers motivations and dynamic experiences to connect with its players.

Working with Streaming Data on AWS

Amazon Web Services (AWS) furnishes a number of alternatives to work with streaming information. You can take advantage of the managed streaming information administrations offered by Amazon Kinesis, or send and deal with your own streaming information arrangement in the cloud on Amazon EC2.

Amazon Kinesis is a stage for spilling information on AWS, offering ground-breaking administrations to make it simple to stack and dissect gushing information, and furthermore empowers you to assemble custom streaming information applications for specific needs. It offers two administrations: Amazon Kinesis Firehose, and Amazon Kinesis Streams.

And, you can run other streaming information stages, for example, – Apache Kafka, Apache Flume, Apache Spark Streaming, and Apache Storm – on Amazon EC2 and Amazon EMR.

Chapter # 19

Amazon Managed Streaming for Apache Kafka

Amazon Managed Streaming for Apache Kafka (Amazon MSK) is a completely managed administration that empowers you to build and run applications that utilization Apache Kafka to process streaming information. Amazon MSK gives the control-plane activities, for example, those for making, refreshing, and deleting clusters. It gives you a chance to utilize Apache Kafka information plane activities, for example, those for delivering and expending information. It runs open-source forms of Apache Kafka. This means existing applications, tooling, and modules from accomplices and the Apache Kafka people group are supported without expecting changes to application code. You can utilize Amazon MSK to make groups that utilization Apache Kafka renditions 1.1.1 and 2.2.1.

The accompanying graph gives an outline of how Amazon MSK functions.

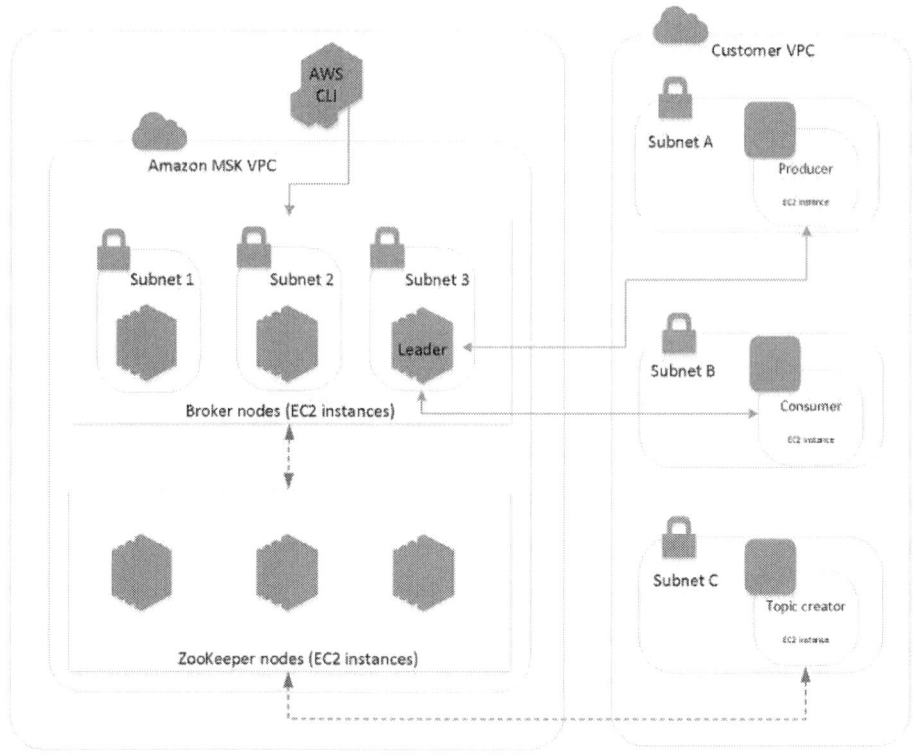

The graph shows the communication between the accompanying segments:

Broker nodes — When making an Amazon MSK bunch, you determine what number of broker nodes you need Amazon MSK to make in every Availability Zone. In the model cluster that appeared in this graph, there's one dealer for each Availability Zone. Every Availability Zone has it's very own virtual private cloud (VPC) subnet.

ZooKeeper nodes — Amazon MSK additionally makes the Apache ZooKeeper hubs for you. Apache ZooKeeper is an open-source server that empowers highly reliable distributed coordination.

Producers, customers, and subject makers — Amazon MSK gives you a chance to utilize Apache Kafka information plane activities to make points and to deliver and consume information.

AWS CLI — you can utilize the AWS Command Line Interface (AWS CLI) or the APIs in the SDK to perform control-plane activities. For instance, you can utilize the AWS CLI or the SDK to make or delete an Amazon MSK group, list every one of the clusters in a record, or view the properties of a group.

Amazon MSK detects and naturally recoups from the most well-known failure situations for Multi-AZ groups so your maker and buyer applications can proceed with their write and read activities with insignificant effect. Amazon MSK naturally identifies the accompanying failure situations:

- Loss of system network to a broker

- Compute unit failure for a broker

At the point when Amazon MSK recognizes one of these failures, it replaces the unfortunate or inaccessible agent with another representative. Furthermore, where possible, it reuses the capacity of the more new broker to decrease the information that Apache Kafka needs to recreate. Your availability impact is constrained to the time required for Amazon MSK to finish the location and recovery. After recovery, your maker and customer applications can keep on speaking with a similar specialist IP tends to that they utilized before the failure.

Advantages

Fully compatible

Amazon MSK runs and managed Apache Kafka for you. This makes it simple for you to relocate and run your current Apache Kafka applications on AWS without changes to the application code. By utilizing Amazon MSK, you keep up open-source similarity and can keep on utilizing recognizable custom and network assembled instruments, for example, MirrorMaker, which gives replication of streams.

Fully managed

Amazon MSK gives you a chance to concentrate on making your streaming applications without stressing over the operational overhead of dealing with your Apache Kafka condition. Amazon MSK deals with the provisioning, setup, and maintenance of Apache Kafka groups and Apache ZooKeeper nodes for you. Amazon MSK additionally shows key Apache Kafka execution measurements in the AWS support.

Highly available

Amazon MSK makes an Apache Kafka group and offers multi-AZ replication inside an AWS Region. Amazon MSK continuously monitors cluster health, and if a part fails, Amazon MSK will consequently replace it.

Highly secure

Amazon MSK gives various degrees of security to your Apache Kafka clusters including VPC organize separation, AWS IAM for control-plane API approval, encryption very still, TLS encryption in-travel, TLS based declaration confirmation, and Apache Kafka Access Control Lists (ACLs) similarity.

How it works

Apache Kafka is a streaming information store that decouples applications producing streaming data (producers) into its information store from applications consuming streaming data (consumers) from its information store. Associations use Apache Kafka as an information source for applications that continuously investigate and respond to streaming information.

Chapter # 20

Amazon Redshift?

Amazon Redshift is a completely managed petabyte-scale cloud-based information distribution center item intended for enormous scale informational collection storage and examination. It is additionally used to perform huge scale database movements.

Redshift's section arranged database is intended to associate with SQL-based customers and business knowledge devices, making information accessible to clients continuously. In light of PostgreSQL 8, Redshift delivers fast performance and proficient questioning that assist groups with settling on sound business investigations and choices.

Every Amazon Redshift data warehouse contains an assortment of computing resources (nodes) sorted out in a cluster. Every Redshift bunch runs its very own Redshift motor and contains at any rate one database.

Amazon Redshift is an immediate option to on-premise customary database distribution centers. How about we take a look at how Redshift piles up to customary warehousing in the accompanying regions:

- Performance

- Cost

- Scalability

- Security

Performance

Amazon Redshift is generally known for its speed. Redshift conveys the quick question speeds on enormous informational collections, managing information evaluates to a petabyte and that's just the beginning. The speed by which Redshift forms information up to these sizes is essentially difficult to achieve in conventional data warehousing, settling on it the top decision for applications that run huge measures of questions on-request.

Cost

Amazon Redshift is notably quicker than traditional warehousing, however with regards to picking tech arrangements, associations are apparently generally worried about cost. As a cloud-based arrangement, Amazon Redshift can give significant level performance affordably. IT officials realize that traditional warehousing is very exorbitant from the earliest starting point, with the underlying expense for equipment perhaps costing up to the multi-millions. Then again, there are no substantial upfront costs to getting the arrangement and off with Redshift. Being a completely managed arrangement, Redshift has no repetitive equipment and support costs. Database administrators can arrangement information distribution centers that can deal with massive amounts of information without experiencing the extensive procedure of obtainment and strategic purchase from the initiative that multi-million-dollar on-premise equipment requires.

Scalability

Redshift takes into consideration greater adaptability and elastic scale. As your necessities change, Redshift can scale up or down in a split second to coordinate your ability and performance needs with a couple of snaps in the administration comfort.

Cost-wise, on-request estimating guarantees you pay for what you use. Not being secured to costly equipment and lengthy support contracts mean associations have the freedom to alter their perspectives without eating up sunk expenses. From a single 160GB DC1. Large node as far as possible up to numerous 16TB DS2.8XLarge nodes for a petabyte or a greater amount of information, you approach preparing power on-request.

Security

Despite the fact that Amazon Redshift is demonstrably superior to traditional warehousing in the previously mentioned respects, security stays to be the tipping point for some enterprises, however, it's not a direct result of known security vulnerabilities. Actually, some still feel worried about not having their information physically present.

Amazon follows the common duty model of security where Amazon is answerable for the security of the cloud, and the association is liable for security in the cloud.

- Security of the cloud: AWS secures the foundation where AWS administrations run in the cloud. They are answerable for ensuring that highlights and administrations that can be utilized safely are accessible to clients. AWS additionally guarantees that security levels are normally tried and checked as a major aspect of AWS consistence.

- Security in the cloud: The security duty of associations utilizing Redshift is dictated by the AWS administration they use. Associations are also responsible for different elements like information sensitivity, an organization's own interior requirements, and consistency with laws and guidelines.

Amazon Redshift Performance

As referenced above, Amazon Redshift can deliver performance with top tier speed because of the utilization of two fundamental engineering components: Massively Parallel Processing (MPP) plan and columnar data storage. We should take a gander at everyone and perceive how they empower quick preparing in Redshift.

Chapter # 21

Fast Data Warehousing

A data warehouse center is a focal storehouse of data that can be broke down to settle on better-educated choices. Data streams into a data warehouse from value-based frameworks, social databases, and different sources, normally on a customary rhythm. Business experts, information researchers, and chiefs get to the information through business intelligence (BI) instruments, SQL customers, and different examination applications. Information and investigation have gotten irreplaceable to organizations to remain competitive. Organizations use reports, dashboards, and investigation instruments to extract bits of knowledge from their information, monitor business performance, and support basic leadership. These reports, dashboards, and examination apparatuses are controlled by information distribution centers, which store information productively to limit I/O and convey inquiry results at blazing rates to hundreds and thousands of clients simultaneously.

Fast query performance through adaptive caching

As associations hope to accelerate time to insight, performance in the area of intuitive queries keeps on being a top necessity. Perhaps the greatest bottleneck and pain focuses on conveying amazing performance is circle get to. This holds particularly valid in distributed computing where the good ways from the process layer to the capacity layer can conceivably differ, prompting problematic question performance. This reserving system prompts faster data access to and at last faster question performances. Notwithstanding smart storing methodologies, Azure SQL DW Compute Optimized Gen2 level currently uses the most recent equipment advancements that Azure offers. Together, the entirety of this empowers Azure SQL DW Compute Optimized Gen2 level to convey the following level of performance qualities. By and large, inquiry outstanding burdens see multiple times the presentation upgrades contrasted with SQL DW Gen1.

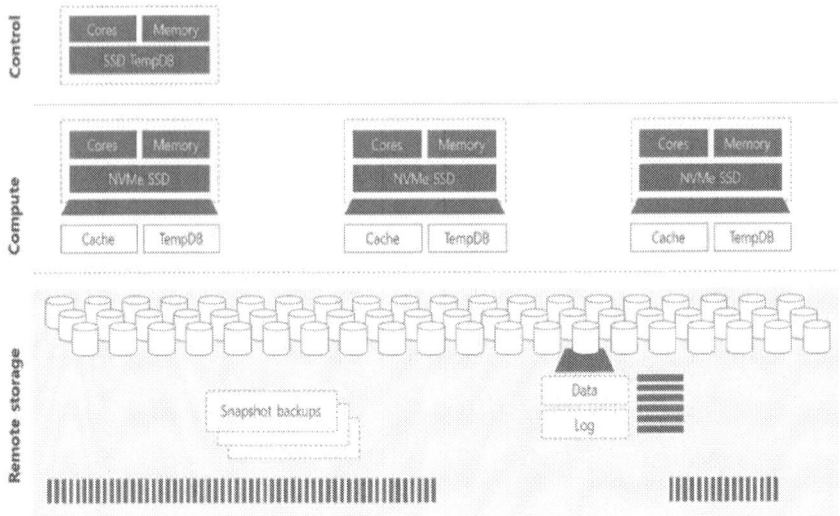

Data Warehouse Architecture

A data warehouse architecture comprises of three tiers. The bottom tier of the design is the database server, where information is loaded and stored. The center tier comprises the investigation engine that is utilized to analyze and access the information. The top-level is the front-end customer that presents results through announcing, examination, and information mining devices.

How Does Data Warehouse Work?

A data warehouse works by sorting out information into a pattern that depicts the design and kind of information, for example, number, data field, or string. At the point when information is ingested, it is put away in different tables described by the diagram. Question devices utilize the diagram to figure out which information tables to get to and examine.

Data Warehouse Benefits

The advantages of a data warehouse are:

- Data quality, consistency, and precision

- Better basic leadership

- Historical intelligence

- Consolidates information from numerous sources

- Separates examination handling from value-based databases, improving the execution of the two frameworks

Get started with Azure SQL Data Warehouse today

Sky blue SQL DW Compute Optimized Gen2 level keeps on offering and support interruption and resume activities, taking into consideration the greatest charging adaptability. We are amped up for carrying this new item age to the market. This offering of multiple times more performance, multiple times more concurrency, and multiple times the extra scale shows we proceeded with a pledge to our clients. Sky blue SQL DW Compute Optimized Gen2 level will turn out to 20 locales at first, you can locate the full list of districts accessible, with resulting rollouts to all other Azure areas. These additions assist make with Azuring SQL Data Warehouse one of the most generally accessible information warehousing arrangements on the planet.

Deploying Your Data Warehouse on AWS

AWS enables you to take advantage the entirety of the center advantages related with on-request figuring, for example, access to apparently limitless storage and register limit, and the capacity to scale your framework in parallel with the developing measure of information gathered put away, and questioned, paying just for the assets your arrangement. Further, AWS offers an expansive arrangement of managed services that coordinate seamlessly with one another so you can rapidly convey a start to finish examination and information warehousing arrangement.

The accompanying representation shows the key steps of a start to finish investigation process chain and the managed services accessible on AWS for each progression:

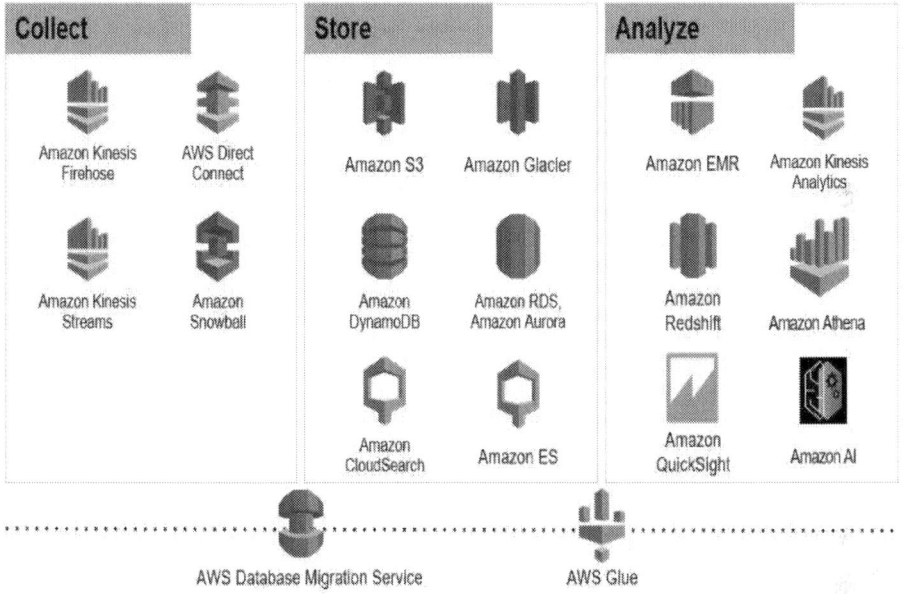

Chapter # 22

Amazon QuickSight

Amazon QuickSight is a business insight apparatus under the umbrella of the Amazon Web Services (AWS) stage. Since its discharge, QuickSight is best known for stunning perceptions, intuitive dashboards, and precise machine learning insight.

Speed is another selling point. Amazon controls the QuickSight stage with its "Super-Fast, Parallel, and In-Memory Calculation Engine "known as" Flavor." According to Amazon:

QuickSight's Visual Presentations

QuickSight is about the visuals. Although progressively costly BI arrangements, like Tableau, have extra representation alternatives as far as amount, the essential visual introductions QuickSight offers are increasingly "beautiful" and "stunning." That offers a good advantage when meeting with customers and clients.

A normal visual introduction on the QuickSight stage is contained in the accompanying parts:

Analyses: QuickSight calls the workspace, where you make and cooperate with visuals an "examination." In this investigation, you can mastermind and align various graphical information introductions, as intuitive diagrams and outlines identifying with performance measurements, deals investigations or cost investigations. You can also incorporate a "story" (see the meaning of "stories" in the last bullet below).

Visuals: A visual is a graphical introduction of information. It could be an outline, table, chart or graph. Recently made visuals start in the "Signature" model. Signature utilizes a calculation to consequently pick visual introductions for the information you select. You would then be able to choose your own perceptions from choices like warmth maps, treemaps, blend diagrams, turntables, and that's just the beginning. You can also change the hues, apply channels and rearrange their positions.

Insights: Insights offer important translations of the information in your "analyses." QuickSight's Enterprise Edition will consequently propose suitable AI experiences and informative introductions, in the wake of analyzing your information.

Sheets: Sheets are groups of visuals that show up on a single page. While setting up an investigation, you'll put the chose visuals into the sheet, like the first page of a paper. Your investigation can incorporate more than one sheet, each with its particular representations cooperating or independently.

Stories: A story enables you to catch various visuals or "scenes" that you present on the sheet, similar to a slideshow. Clients can look through the scenes in the story to see various parts of the investigation. The scenes aren't static, they update progressively like the various diagrams, graphs, and datasets on the dashboard.

Together, the above highlights permit your BI group to make delightful, intuitive information introductions to aid different business areas, for example,

- Managers can utilize them to illuminate their authority choices.

- Sales faculty can likewise utilize them during customer introductions.

- Marketing groups can utilize them to follow the consequences of promoting efforts.

- Accountants can utilize them to screen key financial metrics.

Advantages of Amazon Quicksight

In the wake of assessing the QuickSight stage and discovering what genuine clients think, we distinguished the accompanying focal points of Amazon QuickSight:

Quick Setup and Easy to Use

Your BI group can activate the SPICE engine, incorporate information and start utilizing the QuickSight stage rapidly and effectively, truth be told, a lot faster than other BI stages.

Highly Compatible with Different Data Sources

Coordinating QuickSight with various information sources is simple. The stage incorporates information sources like Amazon Redshift, Amazon Athena, Amazon

S3, Amazon Aurora, Apache Spark, Presto, SQL servers, neighborhood Excel documents, and that's just the beginning. It additionally supports data from administrations like Salesforce and Tableau.

Access Dashboards on Any Web Browser or iOS Device

Most clients will get to QuickSight dashboards and bits of knowledge through a web browser. As indicated by QuickSight, "Amazon QuickSight supports the most recent renditions of Mozilla Firefox, Chrome, Safari, Internet Explorer adaptation 10 or more and Edge." iPhone and iPad clients can also get to and interface with the dashboard by means of their web associated iOS gadgets.

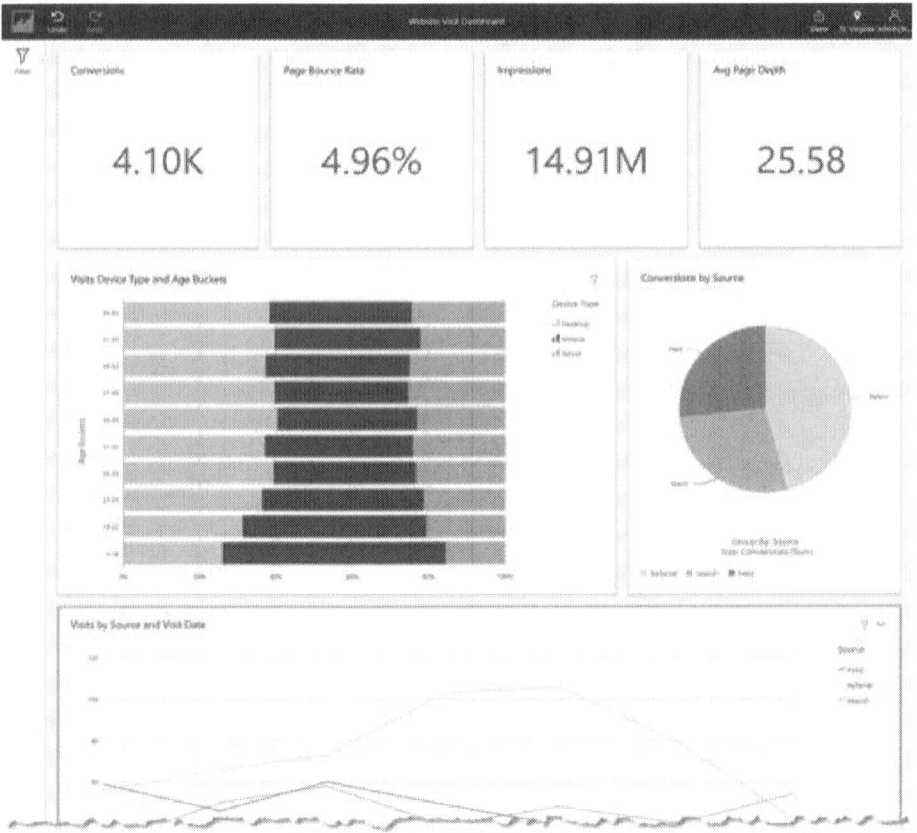

Stunning Visualizations

Compared with different arrangements like Tableau, most clients concur that the quality and introduction of QuickSight's perceptions are superior. Also, QuickSight's "Signature" highlight applies a lot of calculations to find out about your information.

This ETL pipeline process reflects a case of a creative and practical pipeline design that is featured by groups building serverless business intelligence stacks with Apache Parquet, Tableau, and Amazon Athena.

Chapter # 23

What Is the AWS Data Pipeline?

- Deployed inside the conveyed, highly accessible AWS framework

- Provides a simplified comfort inside the AWS interface

- Supports booking, dependency tracking, and error handling

- Distribute work to one machine or numerous

- Billed dependent on use levels, at a monthly rate

- Select the computing resources that execute your ETL or ELT pipeline logic

Why Pipelines Are Important?

Data pipelines are basic to the business. Why? Pause for a minute to consider each one of those frameworks you or your group utilize each day to the interface, impart, draw in, oversee, and delight your clients. These stages spread things like email, social, faithfulness, promoting, portable, web, and a large group of others. The entirety of that data lives in information storehouses. Very frequently this outcome in manual information wrangling as groups attempts to separate those storehouses.

These information extraction and information change forms enable you to move and process information that was recently secured up those remote information storehouses.

A pipeline solves the coordination's between information sources (or frameworks where the information resides) and information purchasers or the individuals who need access to information to attempt further handling, perceptions, changes, routing, reporting or statistical models.

While building up pipelines, you are attempting to decrease friction with ETL or ELT work process, asset accessibility, conditions, transient failures or breaks in singular tasks, or different components. Making a pipeline, including the utilization of the AWS item, settles for complex information handling outstanding tasks at hand needs to close the hole between information sources and information purchasers.

AWS Data Pipeline (or Amazon Data Pipeline) is "infrastructure-as-a-service" web benefits that help to mechanize the vehicle and change of information.

Pipelines mirror an ETL procedure that enables you to get more value from your information over various sources through information extraction and information change downstream to Amazon Web Services, for example, Amazon RDS, Amazon Athena, and Amazon Redshift.

Advantages

Reliable

AWS Data Pipeline is based on a distributed, highly accessible framework intended for deficiency tolerant execution of your exercises. In the event that failures happen in your action rationale or information sources, AWS Data Pipeline consequently retries the action. In the event that the failure persists, AWS Data Pipeline sends you failure notices by means of Amazon Simple Notification Service (Amazon SNS). You can design your warnings for effective runs, delays in arranged exercises, or failures.

Simple to Use

Making a pipeline is quick and simple by means of our simplified reassure. Regular preconditions are incorporated with the administration, so you don't have to write any additional logic to utilize them. For instance, you can check for the presence of an Amazon S3 record by just giving the name of the Amazon S3 basin and the way of the document that you need to check for, and AWS Data Pipeline wraps up. Moreover, its simple visual pipeline maker, AWS Data Pipeline gives a library of pipeline templates. These formats make it easy to make pipelines for various increasingly complex use cases, for example, normally handling your log records, archiving information to Amazon S3, or running intermittent SQL queries.

Flexible

AWS Data Pipeline enables you to take advantage of an assortment of features, for example, booking, dependency tracking, and error dealing with. You can utilize exercises and preconditions that AWS gives as well as write your very own custom ones. This means you can design an AWS Data Pipeline to take activities like run Amazon EMR occupations, execute SQL questions legitimately against databases, or execute custom applications running on Amazon EC2 or in your very own datacenter. This enables you to make ground-breaking custom pipelines to examine and process your information without managing the complexities of dependably booking and executing your application logic.

Chapter # 24

AWS Glue

AWS Glue is a completely managed extract, transform, and loaded (ETL) administration that makes it simple for clients to get ready and lost their information for the investigation. You can make and run an ETL work with a couple of clicks in the AWS Management Console. You basically point AWS Glue to your information put away on AWS, and AWS Glue finds your information and stores the related metadata (for example table definition and construction) in the AWS Glue Data Catalog. Once listed, your information is quickly accessible, queryable, and accessible for ETL.

Benefits

Less hassle

AWS Glue is incorporated over a wide scope of AWS administrations, which means less issue for you while onboarding. AWS Glue locally supports information put away in Amazon Aurora and all other Amazon RDS motors, Amazon Redshift, and Amazon S3, just as basic database engines and databases in your Virtual Private Cloud (Amazon VPC) running on Amazon EC2.

Cost-effective

AWS Glue is serverless. There is no foundation for the arrangement or manage. AWS Glue handles provisioning, arrangement, and scaling of the assets required to run your ETL employments on a completely managed, scale-out Apache Spark condition. You pay just for the assets utilized while your occupations are running.

More power

AWS Glue robotizes a significant part of the effort in building, keeping up, and running ETL occupations. AWS Glue crawls your information sources, distinguishes information organizes and suggests patterns and changes. AWS Glue consequently produces the code to execute your information changes and loading forms.

How did it work?

Select an information source and information target. AWS Glue will create ETL code in Scala or Python to separate information from the source, change the information to coordinate the objective outline and burden it into the objective. You can alter, investigate and test this code by means of the Console, in your most loved IDE, or any scratchpad.

Stage 1: Build your Data Catalog

To start with, utilize the AWS Management Console to register your information sources. AWS Glue will crawl your information sources and develop your Data Catalog utilizing pre-constructed classifiers for some, mainstream source arrangements and information types, including JSON, CSV, Parquet, and more.

Stage 2: Generate and Edit Transformations

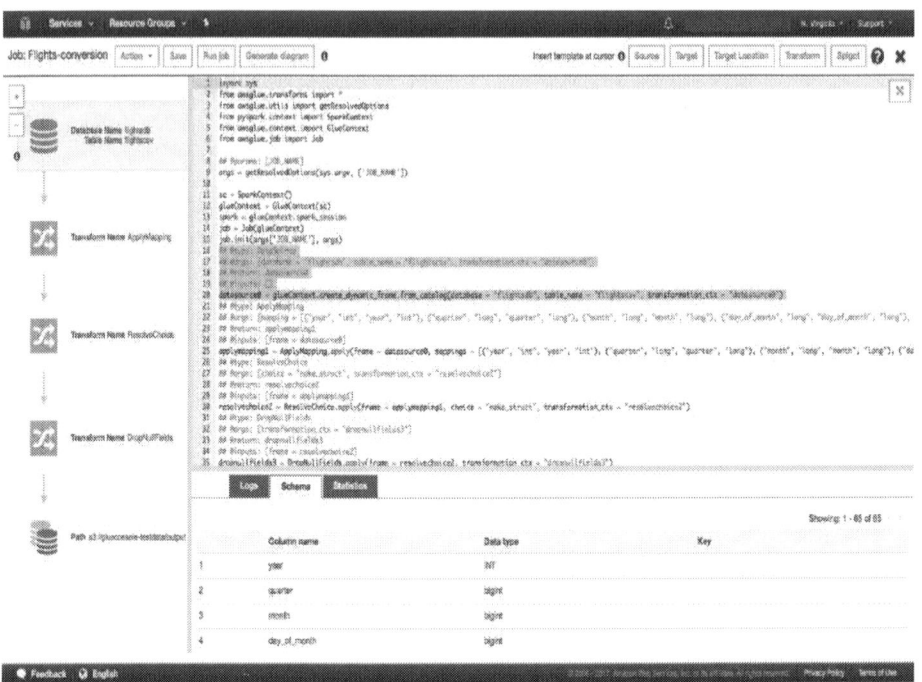

Next, select an information source and information target. AWS Glue will produce ETL code in Scala or Python to remove information from the source, change the information to coordinate the objective composition and burden it into the objective. You can alter, debug and test this code by means of the Console, in your most loved IDE, or any notebook.

Stage 3: Schedule and Run Your Jobs

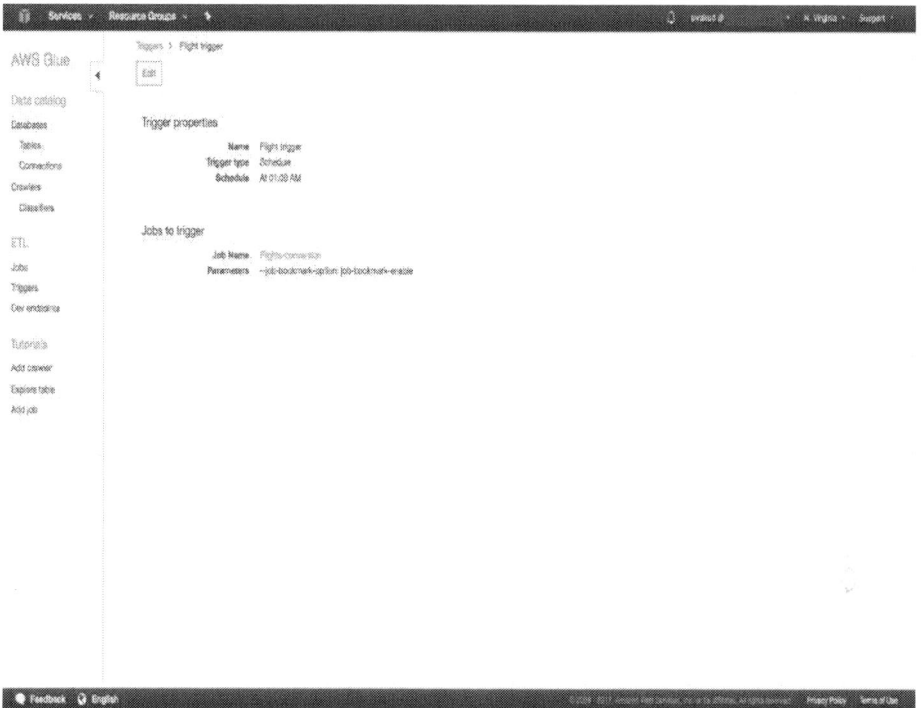

AWS Glue makes it simple to plan to repeat ETL occupations, chain various employments together, or summon employments on-request from different administrations like AWS Lambda. AWS Glue deals with the conditions between your employments, consequently scales underlying assets, and retries jobs if they fail.

According to Amazon, there are numerous conceivable use cases for AWS Glue to streamline ETL tasks, including:

- Discovering metadata about your different databases and information stores, and chronicling them in the AWS Glue Data Catalog.

- Creating ETL contents so as to change, denormalize, and advance the information while in transit from source to target.

- Automatically identifying changes in your database pattern and modifying the administration so as to coordinate them.

- Launching ETL employments dependent on a specific trigger, timetable, or occasion.

- Collecting logs, measurements, and KPIs on your ETL activities for observing and detailing purposes.

- Handling errors and retrying so as to avoid slowing down during the procedure.

- Scaling assets naturally so as to fit the requirements of your present circumstance.

AWS Glue: Features and Functionality

The significant features of AWS Glue include:

Serverless computing: AWS Glue is a serverless offering, which implies that you don't need to physically assign a server to run it. At whatever point you need to utilize AWS Glue usefulness, Amazon turns up a server for you and afterward closes it down when it's never again being used. This programmed provisioning frees you from the task of overseeing or scaling the foundation yourself.

Apache Spark: AWS Glue depends on the Apache Spark examination motor for enormous information preparing. Be that as it may, the administration additionally enables clients to make content in Python and Scala.

Chapter # 25

Aws lake formation:

AWS Lake Formation is assistance that makes it simple to set up a protected information lake in days. An information lake is an incorporated, curated, and secured repository that stores every one of your information, both in its unique structure and arranged for investigation. An information lake enables you to separate information storehouses and join various kinds of investigation to pick up bits of knowledge and guide better business choices.

In any case, setting up and overseeing information lakes today includes a great deal of manual, confounded, and tedious errands. This work incorporates loading information from diverse sources, observing those information streams, setting up parcels, turning on encryption and overseeing keys, characterizing change employments and checking their activity, re-arranging information into a columnar arrangement, configuring access control settings, deduplication redundant information, coordinating connected records, allowing access to informational collections, and reviewing access after some time. The Resource segment demonstrates whether each activity supports asset level consents. If there is no incentive for this segment, you should indicate all assets ("*") in the Resource component of your arrangement proclamation. If the segment incorporates an asset type, at that point you can indicate an ARN of that type in an announcement with that activity. Required assets are demonstrated in the table with an asterisk (*).

Making an information lake with Lake Formation is as basic as characterizing information sources and what information access and security arrangements you need to apply. Lake Formation at that point encourages you to gather and inventory information from databases and article storage, move the information into your new Amazon S3 information lake, clean and group your information utilizing AI calculations, and secure access to your touchy information. Your clients can get to an incorporated information inventory that describes accessible informational collections and their appropriate utilization. Your clients at that point influence these informational collections with their decision of examination and AI administrations, similar to Amazon Redshift, Amazon Athena, and (in beta) Amazon EMR for Apache Spark. Lake Formation expands on the capacities accessible in AWS Glue.

Advantages

Build data lakes quickly

With Lake Formation, you can move, store, list, and clean your information quicker. You essentially point Lake Formation at your information sources, and Lake Formation creeps those sources and moves the information into your new Amazon S3 information lake. Lake Formation arranges information in S3 around every now and again utilized inquiry terms and into right-sized chunks to expand productivity. Lake Formation additionally changes information into designs like Apache Parquet and ORC for faster analytics. Moreover, Lake Formation has worked in AI to duplicate and find coordinating records (two passages that allude to something very similar) to expand information quality.

Simplify security management

You can utilize Lake Formation to midway characterize security, administration, and examining approaches in a single spot, as opposed to carrying out these responsibilities per administration, and later authorize those strategies for your clients over their investigation applications. Your strategies are reliably executed, taking out the need to physically design them across security administrations like AWS Identity and Access Management and AWS Key Management Service, storage services like S3, and examination and AI administrations like Redshift, Athena, and (in beta) EMR for Apache Spark. This decreases the effort in configuring policies across services and gives reliable implementation and consistency.

Provide self-service access to data

With Lake Formation you assemble an information index that describes the various informational indexes that are accessible alongside which groups of clients approach each. This makes your clients increasingly beneficial by helping them locate the correct informational collection to investigate. By providing a catalog of your information with a steady security requirement, Lake Formation makes it simpler for your examiners and information researchers to utilize their favored analytics service.

They can utilize EMR for Apache Spark (in beta), Redshift, or Athena on differing informational collections presently housed in a single information lake. Clients can also join these administrations without moving information between storehouses.

How does it work?

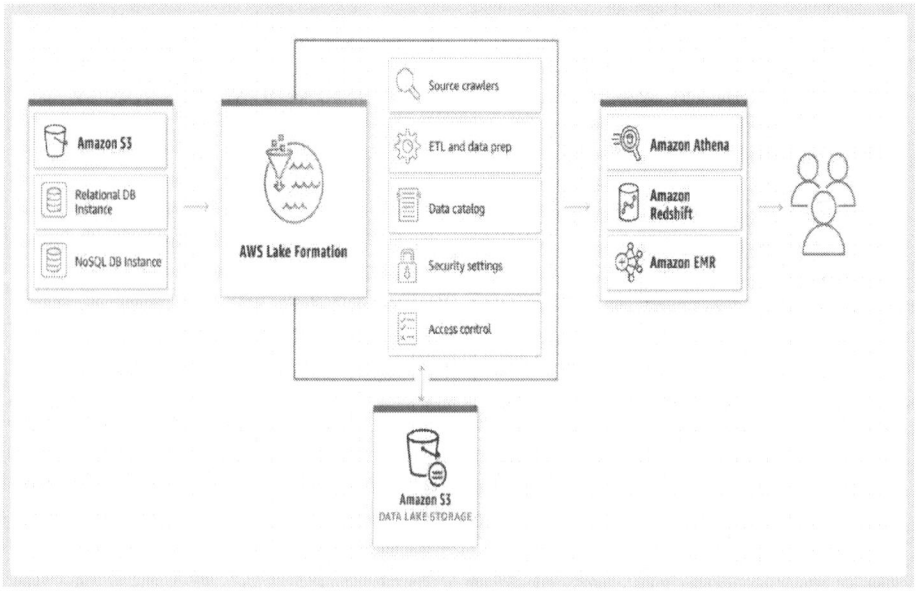

Lake Formation assembles, secure, and deal with your information lake. To start with, distinguish existing information stores in S3 or social and NoSQL databases, and move the information into your information lake. Then crawl, catalog, and set up the information for the investigation. At that point give your clients secure self-service access to the information through their decision of analytics services. Different AWS services and outsider applications can also get to information through the services that appeared. Lake Formation deals with the entirety of the assignments in the orange box and is coordinated with the information stores and administrations that appeared in the blue boxes.

Chapter # 26

Aws certified solution architect

The AWS Solutions Architect – Associate Certification (or Sol Arch Associate for short) offers some reasonable advantages:

- Increases marketability to employers

- Provides strong credentials in a developing industry (with anticipated development of as much as 70 percent in five years)

- Market examination shows it is the most lucrative AWS IT accreditation in 2019. If the AWS Solutions Architect – Associate is your next confirmation, you're most likely wondering where to begin in your planning. What do you have to learn? To what extent will it take? Try not to stress. At Cloud Academy, we have you secured with this total AWS Certified Solutions Architect – Associate investigation direct. Our Learning Path contains all that you have to know for this confirmation, sorted out bit by bit. This article explains how to utilize our Learning Paths, and how much time it takes to get ready for the test.

AWS Certified Solutions Architect – Associate examination direct: What is a Learning Path?

Cloud Academy offers a wide variety of video courses, tests, and Hands-on Labs on various zones of cloud computing. Our Learning Paths assist you with getting from where you are to where you need to go. The Sol Arch partner learning way is basically your AWS affirmed Solutions Architect – Associate study guide.

Our Solutions Architect – Associate Learning Path contains the entirety of the courses, labs, and tests you have to assist you to pass the AWS certification test.

Each sort of content on the Learning Path fills an alternate instructional need:

- Video courses give guided talks on key areas of the test, with models.

- The Hands-on Labs give direct access to the AWS administration test areas.

- Quizzes are the chance to show what you've realized, with connections to AWS documentation.

The Solutions Architect – Associate Learning Path focuses on:

- Designing exceptionally accessible, cost-productive, fault-tolerant and scalable frameworks

- Implementation and arrangement

- Data security

- Troubleshooting

Using the Learning Path

A fundamental component of the AWS Certified Solutions Architect – Associate study manage includes understanding the gaps in your insight. To begin with, think about what you definitely know and what you have to know. Where do you have involvement with registering or working with cloud services? What essential cloud service types (IaaS, PaaS or SaaS, for instance) would you say you are generally familiar with? How does this set you up for the Solutions Architect test? Second, take a look at the general information essentials. The main earlier information prescribed for this Learning Path is fundamental recognition with center AWS capacities. If you know these capacities, at that point you are prepared. (If you are new to AWS, or need a boost, start with the Fundamentals of AWS Learning Path first).

Third, the Solutions Architect – Associate Learning Path normally works from AWS essentials to further developed areas. For the best approach, start toward the start with the principal course and proceed with bit by bit. Complete every action so as to guarantee that you're comfortable with administrations like EC2 or DynamoDB. At that point, proceed onward to test your insight into the labs and tests.

There is no mystery. Simply ensure that you comprehend the essentials of AWS, and go from that point.

How long will it take?

This is a natural question. Passing the test requires being strong and steady, and to what extent that takes relies upon where you start.

All things considered, we suggest roughly 80 hours of arrangement for the Solution Architect – Associate Exam, as long as you have some AWS experience. This incorporates study over the entirety of your assets, including our Solutions Architect Learning Path, and whatever other assets that you pick. (Here you will discover more counsel and prescribed study assets for the Solutions Architect – Associate Certification). With an all-day work and different duties, contributing 80 hours of study, for the most part, takes two months.

In the event that you are completely new to AWS, we suggest roughly 120 hours or three months get ready. Start with the basics, and later move to the Solutions Architect – Associate Learning Path.

Where to focus your time?

What amount of the Solutions Architect – Associate test interfaces with your present or past work understanding? This will give you a thought of where to focus your time on adapting new points. We'll examine a few basics, and I highly prescribe this online class where two experienced experts give understanding into setting yourself up for accreditation tests.

Around 60 percent of the Solutions Architect – Associate Exam centers on Designing Solutions. In the event that you work in Solutions Design or Architecture, or if your job incorporates these duties, these subjects, ideas, and administrations may as of now be familiar to you.

Chapter # 27

Amazon glacier

Amazon S3 Glacier and S3 Glacier Deep Archive are protected, durable, and very minimal effort Amazon S3 cloud storage classes for data archiving and long-term backup. They are intended to convey 99.999999999% durability and give exhaustive security and consistency abilities that can assist meet even the most stringent administrative prerequisites. Clients can store information for as meager as $1 per terabyte every month, critical investment fund contrasted with on-premises requirements. To minimize expenses yet appropriate for shifting recovery needs, Amazon S3 Glacier gives three choices to access to documents, from a couple of moments to a few hours, and S3 Glacier Deep Archive gives two access alternatives going from 12 to 48 hours.

Advantages

Recoveries AS QUICK AS 1-5 MINUTES

The Amazon S3 Glacier storage class gives three recovery choices to accommodate your utilization case. Expedited recoveries normally return information in 1-5 minutes, and are incredible for Active Archive use cases. Standard recoveries ordinarily complete between 3-5 hours, and function admirably for less time-sensitive needs like backup information, media editing, or long-term investigation. Mass recoveries are the most reduced cost recovery choice, returning a lot of information inside 5-12 hours. The Amazon S3 Glacier Deep Archive storage class gives two recovery alternatives running from 12-48 hours.

UNMATCHED DURABILITY & SCALABILITY

The Amazon S3 Glacier and S3 Glacier Deep Archive storage classes run on the worlds biggest worldwide cloud foundation and were intended for 99.999999999% of durability. Information is consequently circulated over at least three physical Availability Zones that are topographically separated inside an AWS Region.

MOST COMPREHENSIVE SECURITY and COMPLIANCE CAPABILITIES

The Amazon S3 Glacier and S3 Glacier Deep Archive storage classes offer a complex mix with AWS CloudTrail to log, screen and hold storage API call exercises for auditing, and supports three unique types of encryption. These capacity classes also support security models and consistence confirmations including SEC Rule 17a-4, PCI-DSS, HIPAA/HITECH, FedRAMP, EU GDPR, and FISMA, and Amazon S3 Object Lock empowers WORM stockpiling abilities, fulfilling consistency necessities for practically every administrative office around the world.

LOW COST

Amazon S3 Glacier and S3 Glacier Deep Archive are intended to be the most minimal cost Amazon S3 storage classes, enabling you to chronicle a lot of information requiring little to no effort. This makes it practical to hold every one of the information you need for use cases like information lakes, examination, IoT, AI, consistence, and media resource documenting. You pay just for what you need, with no base responsibilities or direct front expenses.

MOST SUPPORTED BY PARTNERS, VENDORS, & AWS SERVICES

Moreover, combined with most AWS administrations, Amazon S3 object storage services incorporate a huge number of counseling, frameworks integrator, and autonomous programming seller accomplices, with all the more joining each month. AWS Partner Network accomplices have adjusted their services and programming to work with Amazon S3 storage classes for arrangements like Backup and Recovery, Archiving, and Disaster Recovery. No other cloud supplier has more bands together with arrangements that are pre-incorporated to work with their administration.

Use cases

MEDIA ASSET WORKFLOWS

Media resources, for example, video and news films require strong stockpiling and can develop too numerous petabytes after some time. The Amazon S3 Glacier and S3 Glacier Deep Archive storage classes enable you to document more established media content moderately then move it to Amazon S3 for circulation when required.

HEALTHCARE INFORMATION ARCHIVING

Medical clinic frameworks need to hold petabytes of patient records (LIS, PACS, EHR, and so forth.) for a considerable length of time to meet administrative necessities. The Amazon S3 Glacier and S3 Glacier Deep Archive storage classes help you dependably chronicle quiet record information safely at an exceptionally minimal effort.

Administrative AND COMPLIANCE ARCHIVING

Numerous organizations like Financial Services and Healthcare must hold administrative and consistence documents for expanded lengths. Amazon S3 Object Lock causes you set consistence controls to meet your destinations, for example, SEC Rule 17a-4(f).

Logical DATA STORAGE

Research organizations produce, archive, and analyze huge measures of information. With the Amazon S3 Glacier and S3 Glacier Deep Archive storage classes, you evade the complexities of equipment and office the executives and capacity planning.

DIGITAL PRESERVATION

Libraries and government organizations face data-integrity challenges in their advanced protection endeavors. In contrast to conventional frameworks, which can require relentless information confirmation and manual fix, Amazon S3 performs ordinary, efficient information data-integrity checks and is worked to be consequently self-healing.

Chapter # 28

Amazon machine learning

Welcome to the Amazon Machine Learning Developer Guide. Amazon Machine Learning (Amazon ML) is a robust, cloud-based assistance that makes it simple for designers of all ability levels to utilize AI innovation. Amazon ML gives representation tools and wizards that guide you through the way toward making machine learning (ML) models without learning complex ML calculations and innovation. When your models are prepared, Amazon ML makes it simple to get forecasts for your application utilizing basic APIs, without actualizing custom expectation age code, or deal with any framework. The Machine Learning world today is quickly turning out to be democratized, with arrangements accessible to any organization, paying little respect to data science expertise. Regardless of whether you utilize a committed data science group or are totally new to machine learning and data science, arrangements from AWS and AWS Partner Network

(APN) Partners can assist you with profiting by the intensity of machine learning innovation.

How AWS looks at machine learning

Machine learning (ML) refers to the utilization of learning calculations that build a model of comprehension about the connections between existing information to make expectations about new information. The term is frequently utilized conversely with artificial intelligence (AI), however, in truth, these terms refer to related, yet separated, ideas. Artificial intelligence is the capacity to detect, learn, reason, act, and adjust to this present reality without express programming. Artificial intelligence is the general idea of building arrangements that enable PCs to learn and settle on choices without specific programming, and ML is the technique by which engineers make those capacities. Deep learning (DL) is the third term regularly utilized when talking about AI. As opposed to utilizing specific numerical calculations, DL attempts to demonstrate how the mind functions and learns with frameworks called neural systems. DL is a viable device to utilize when the arrangement is difficult to articulate.

For instance, concisely clarifying how we distinguish a dog from every single other article and animals is uncommonly troublesome. Moreover, with DL we can have the neural system train itself what a dog is through assessment and input, like how a kid figures out how to recognize dogs.

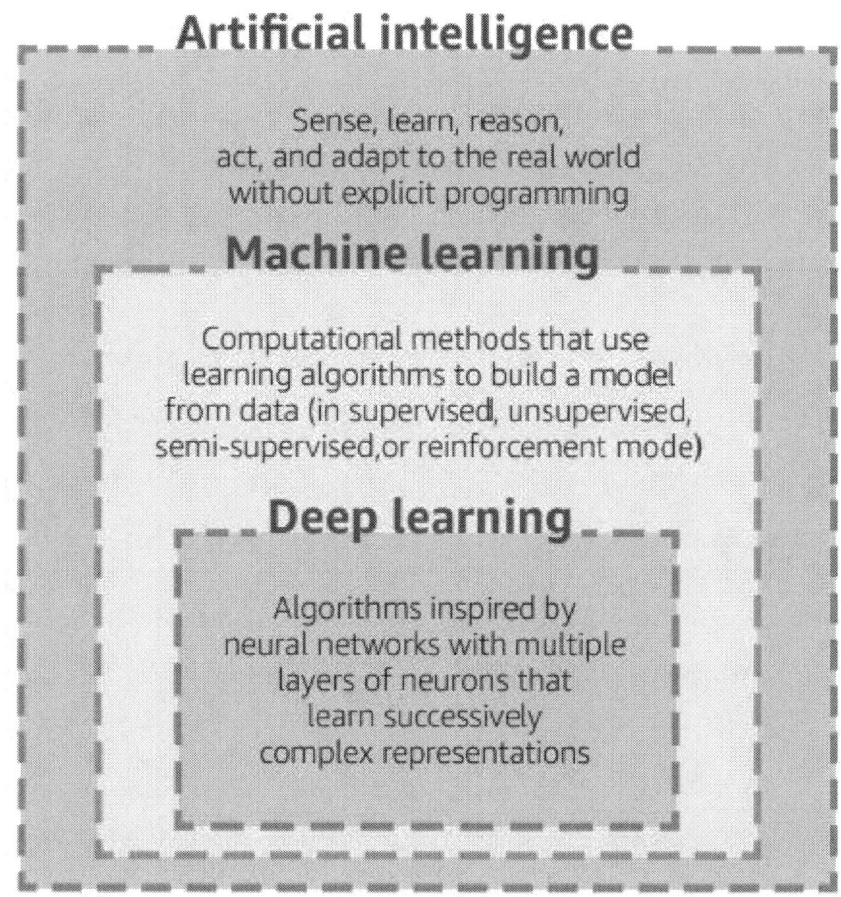

Artificial intelligence

Sense, learn, reason,
act, and adapt to the real world
without explicit programming

Machine learning

Computational methods that use
learning algorithms to build a model
from data (in supervised, unsupervised,
semi-supervised, or reinforcement mode)

Deep learning

Algorithms inspired by
neural networks with multiple
layers of neurons that
learn successively
complex representations

Advantages of AWS for machine learning

AWS gives a scalable, flexible, and cost-effective stage for building, preparing, and facilitating AI and AI applications. Amazing process assets including the most dominant GPU-based occasions in the cloud, to make model preparing and induction quick and proficient.

- Support for every single significant structure including Apache MXNet and Gluon, TensorFlow, Microsoft Cognitive Toolkit, Caffe, Caffe2, Theano, Torch, PyTorch, Chainer, and Keras.

- Flexibility to send ML models in Amazon EC2 cases, Amazon Lambda, on FPGA (on F1 occasion types), or even in an edge utilizing AWS Greengrass.

- Deep ML ability from a huge number of Amazon engineers who have created ML answers for the Amazon.com retail site, Amazon Alexa, Amazon Go, and numerous different regions over the organization.

- Security, including a wide cluster of access control, personality the executives, and encryption capacities.

- Platform mixes, including integrations for the information lake and database tools you have to run ML workloads.

- Comprehensive examination services including information warehousing, business knowledge, bunch handling, stream preparing, and information work process coordination to increase ML applications.

Explore AWS machine learning services

Deploying on AWS enables associations to adjust and enhance all the more rapidly. AWS offers clients the capacity to store and break down petabyte-scale informational indexes, utilizing just the assets they need, and paying just for what they devour. AWS administrations empower associations to manufacture and send cloud-based AI arrangements that can:

Prepare informational indexes for investigation by AI models

Develop, test, send, and improve AI models

Deploy end-client AI answers for explicit use cases

Amazon Sage Maker

Construct, train, and send AI models at scale

Amazon Rekognition

Deep learning-based picture and video examination

Amazon Transcribe

The programmed, grammatically right interpretation of speech

Amazon Lex

Include voice and talk conversational bots to your applications

Amazon Polly

Transform content into similar speech across numerous languages

Amazon Deep Lens

A completely programmable camera, instructional exercises, code, and pre-prepared models intended to grow profound learning skills.

Amazon Comprehend

Discover insights and connections in content

Amazon Deep Learning AMIs

Pre-designed conditions to rapidly fabricate deep learning applications

Amazon Translate

Regular and familiar language interpretation

The AWS Machine Learning Competency

AWS Machine Learning Competency Partners give arrangements that assist associations with tackling their information challenges, empower AI and information science work processes, or offer SaaS-based abilities that upgrade end applications with machine knowledge. Admission to the AWS Machine Learning Competency is highly focused, and prospective Partners are required to experience a thorough inspecting procedure to be admitted to the program. These Partners have been successful in showing high expertise in Machine Learning on AWS and the capacity to convey their association's answers flawlessly on AWS.

Chapter # 29

AWS Budgets

AWS Budgets enables you to set custom spending plans that alarm you when your expenses or usage exceed (or are anticipated to exceed) your planned sum. You can also utilize AWS Budgets to set reservation use or inclusion targets and get alarms when your usage drops under the edge you characterize. Reservation alarms are supported for Amazon EC2, Amazon RDS, Amazon Redshift, Amazon ElastiCache, and Amazon Elasticsearch reservations.

AWS Budgets Dashboard

The AWS Budgets Dashboard is your center point for making, following, and examining your inspecting your limits. From the AWS Budgets Dashboard, you can make, alter, and deal with your financial limits, just as view the status of every one of your spending limits. You can also see extra insights regarding your financial limits, for example, a high-level variance investigation and a spending criteria list.

Budgets can be made at the month to month, quarterly, or yearly level, and you can modify the beginning and end dates. You can additionally refine your spending limit to follow costs related to different measurements, for example, AWS administration, connected record, tag, and others. Budget alerts can be sent by means of email as well as the Amazon Simple Notification Service (SNS) point.

AWS Budgets Reports

AWS Budgets Reports enable you to make and send day by day, week by week, or month to month reports to look at the performance of your AWS Budgets. Utilizing the

AWS Budgets Reports comfort, you can easily choose the subset of budgets that you might want to remember for your report, characterize the delivery frequency, and indicate up to 50 email clients.

Each AWS Budgets Report conveyed through email will acquire an expense of $0.01.

Creating a Cost Budget

Utilize this strategy to make a cost-based spending plan.

To make a cost budget

1. Sign in to the AWS Management Console and open the Billing and Cost Management support at https://console.aws.amazon.com/charging/home #/.

2. In the navigation sheet, pick Budgets.

3. At the highest point of the page, pick Create a budget.

4. For Select budget type, pick Cost budget plan.

5. Choose Set up your financial limit.

6. For Name, enter the name of your financial limit. Your budget name must be extraordinary inside your record and can utilize A-Z, a-z, spaces, and the accompanying characters:

   _.:/=+-%@

7. For Period, pick how regularly you need the budget allowance to reset the real and determined spend. Pick Monthly for consistently, Quarterly for at regular intervals, and annually for consistently. You can also set custom future planned sums for Monthly and Quarterly by utilizing the Budget Planning feature.

8. For a fixed Budgeted Amount, enter the aggregate sum that you need to spend on this spending period. For Monthly and Quarterly Planning budget plans, enter the sum you need to spend on each arranged period.

Note

After the entirety of the Budgeted Amounts esteems in Planned Budget are utilized, the spending keeps on utilizing as far as possible as the Budgeted Amount. By then, the arranged budget plan gives a similar encounter as a fixed budget plan.

9. (Optional) For Budget successful dates, pick Recurring Budget for spending that resets after the budget time frame or Expiring Budget for one-time spending that doesn't reset after the budget time frame.

For Start Month, pick the month that you need the monetary allowance to begin on.

For an Expiring Budget, for End Month, pick the month that you need the budget allowance to end on.

All budget occasions are in UTC.

10. (Optional) Under Budget parameters (optional), for Filtering, pick at least one of the accessible channels. Your decision of budget type decides the arrangement of channels that are shown on the comfort.

11. (Optional) Under Budget parameters (optional), for Advanced alternatives, pick at least one of the accompanying channels. In the event

that you are marked in from a part account in an association rather than from a master account, you probably won't see the entirety of the advanced choices.

Refunds

Any refunds that you got.

Credits

Any AWS credits that are applied to your record.

Upfront reservation charges

Any upfront expenses that are charged to your record. At the point when you buy an All Upfront or Partial Upfront Reserved Instance from AWS, you pay an upfront charge in return for a lower rate for utilizing the instance.

Repeating reservation charges

Any common charges to your record. At the point when you buy a Partial Upfront or No Upfront Reserved Instance from AWS, you pay a repetitive charge in return for a lower rate for utilizing the occasion.

Chapter # 30

Amazon Managed Blockchain

Amazon Managed Blockchain is a completely managed service that makes it simple to make and manage adaptable blockchain systems utilizing the well-known open-source structures Hyperledger Fabric and Ethereum*. Blockchain causes it conceivable to assemble applications where numerous teams can execute exchanges without the requirement for a trusted, central authority. Today, building a scalable blockchain coordinate with existing advancements is unpredictable to set up and difficult to manage. To make a blockchain organize, each system part needs to physically arrangement equipment, introduce programming, make and oversee authentications forget to control, and design organizing segments. Once the blockchain arranges is running, you have to consistently screen the foundation and adjust to changes, for example, an expansion in exchange demands, or new individuals joining or leaving the system.

Amazon Managed Blockchain is a completely managed service that enables you to set up and deal with a scalable blockchain coordinate with only a couple of clicks. Amazon Managed Blockchain wipes out the overhead required to make the system and naturally scales to satisfy the needs of thousands of utilizations running a large number of exchanges. When your system is going, Managed Blockchain makes it simple to manage and keep up your blockchain organize. It deals with your certificates and lets you effectively welcome new individuals to join the system. A model is a retail client hoping to associate its providers with a brought together record that keeps up a simple and obvious history of data identified with the development of an item through its store network. In the other case, various groups execute in a decentralized way without the requirement for an incorporated, trusted authority. A model is a consortium of banks and fare houses hoping to perform a cross-limit move of advantages (for example letter-of-credits) among one another, without a brought together power going about as a contact.

Begin with Hyperledger Fabric utilizing Amazon Managed Blockchain here.

For applications that need a permanent and undeniable record database, visit Amazon QLDB here.

Hyperledger Fabric accessible today. Ethereum just around the corner.

Reporting Amazon Managed Blockchain

Advantages

Completely managed

With Amazon Managed Blockchain, you can rapidly make blockchain systems that range various AWS accounts, empowering a gathering of individuals to execute exchanges and offer information without a central authority. Not at all like self-facilitating your blockchain framework, Amazon Managed Blockchain disposes of the requirement for physically provisioning equipment, designing programming, and setting up systems administration and security segments. With Managed Blockchain's voting API, network participants can cast a ballot to include or evacuate individuals. When another part is included, Managed Blockchain allows that to part dispatch and design numerous blockchain peer hubs to process exchange asks for and store a duplicate of the record. Overseen Blockchain also screens the system and consequently replaces ineffectively performing nodes.

Choice of Hyperledger Fabric or Ethereum

Amazon Managed Blockchain bolsters two prominent blockchain structures, Hyperledger Fabric and Ethereum. Hyperledger Fabric is appropriate for applications that require stringent security and consent controls with a known arrangement of individuals, for instance, a budgetary application where certain exchange related information is just mutual with select banks. Ethereum is appropriate for highly distributed blockchain systems where transparency of information for all individuals is significant, for instance, a client devotion blockchain organizes that enables any retailer in the system to freely check a client's action overall individuals to recover benefits. On the other hand, Ethereum can also be utilized for joining an open Ethereum blockchain organize.

Scalable and Secure

Amazon Managed Blockchain can without much of a stretch scale your blockchain organize as the utilization of uses on the system develops after some time. At the point when a system part requires extra limit with regards to making and approving exchanges, the part can rapidly include another peer node utilizing Managed Blockchain's APIs. Managed Blockchain gives a determination of occurrence types that contain changing combinations of CPU and memory to give you the adaptability to pick the suitable combination of assets for your outstanding task at hand. Moreover, Managed Blockchain protects your system's endorsements with AWS Key Management Service (KMS) innovation, eliminating the requirement for you to set up your own safe key storage.

How it works

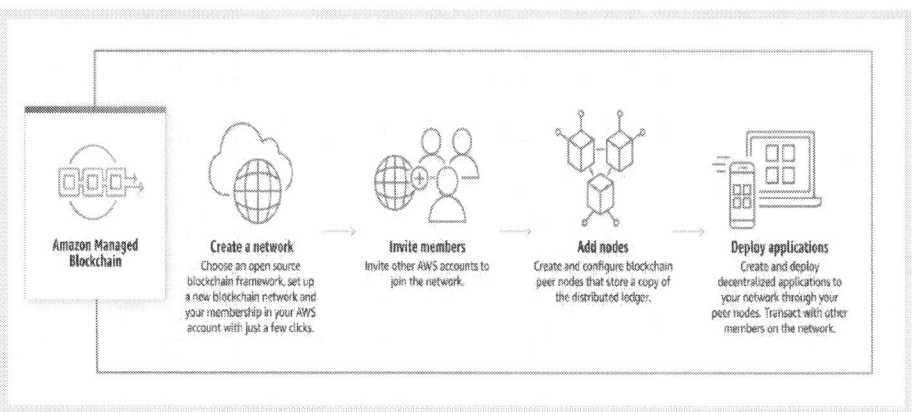

Amazon Managed Blockchain

Create a network
Choose an open source blockchain framework, set up a new blockchain network and your membership in your AWS account with just a few clicks.

Invite members
Invite other AWS accounts to join the network.

Add nodes
Create and configure blockchain peer nodes that store a copy of the distributed ledger.

Deploy applications
Create and deploy decentralized applications to your network through your peer nodes. Transact with other members on the network.

Chapter # 31

AWS Lambda

AWS Lambda (or Lambda for short) is a serverless computing service given by AWS. In this section, we will be utilizing Lambda to build our serverless application. And keeping in mind that we don't have to manage the internals of how Lambda functions, it's critical to have a general thought of how your capacities will be executed.

Lambda Specs

We should begin by rapidly taking a look at the specialized particulars of AWS Lambda. Lambda underpins the accompanying runtimes.

- Node.js: v10.15 and v8.10

- Java 8

- Python: 3.7, 3.6, and 2.7

- .NET Core: 1.0.1 and 2.1

- Go 1.x

- Ruby 2.5

- Rust

Each capacity runs inside a holder with a 64-piece Amazon Linux AMI. And, the execution condition has:

- Memory: 128MB - 3008MB, in 64 MB increases

- Ephemeral circle space: 512MB

- Max execution span: 900 seconds

- Compressed bundle size: 50MB

- Uncompressed bundle size: 250MB

You may see that CPU isn't referenced as a piece of the container determination. This is on the grounds that you can't control the CPU directly. As you increment the memory, the CPU is expanded also.

The vaporous disk space is accessible as the/tmp index. You can just utilize this space for impermanent storage since subsequent invocations won't approach this. We'll talk more about the stateless idea of the Lambda capacities below.

The execution term means that your Lambda capacity can run for a limit of 900 seconds or 15 minutes. This implies Lambda isn't intended for long-running procedures.

The bundle size refers to all your code important to run your capacity. This incorporates any conditions (node_modules/catalog if there should arise an occurrence of Node.js) that your capacity may import. There is an utmost of 250MB on the uncompressed bundle and a 50MB limit once it has been compacted. We'll investigate the packaging procedure below.

Lambda Function

At long last here is the thing that a Lambda work (a Node.js rendition) resembles.

Here **myHandler** is the name of our Lambda work. The **event** object contains all the data about the occasion that set off this Lambda. On account of an HTTP demand, it'll be data about the particular HTTP demand. The **context** object contains information about the runtime our Lambda work is executing in. After we do practically everything inside our Lambda work, we essentially call the **callback** function with the outcomes (or the blunder) and AWS will react to the HTTP demand with it.

Packaging Functions

Lambda functions should be bundled and sent to AWS. This is typically a procedure of compacting the capacity and every one of its conditions and transferring it to an S3 bucket. Also, letting AWS realize that you need to utilize this bundle when a particular occasion happens. To assist us with this procedure we utilize the Serverless Framework. We'll go over this in detail later on in this guide.

Execution Model

The container (and the assets utilized by it) that runs our capacity is managed totally by AWS. It is raised when an occasion happens and is turned off if it isn't being utilized. If extra demands are made while the first occasion is being served, another compartment is raised to serve a request. This means if we are experiencing a utilization spike, the cloud supplier essentially makes various cases of the holder with our capacity to serve those requests.

This makes them interesting suggestions. Initially, our capacities are adequately stateless. Also, each request (or occasion) is served by a single case of a Lambda work. This means you won't deal with simultaneous demands in your code. AWS raises a compartment at whatever point there is another request. It makes a few advancements here. It will hold tight to the compartment for a couple of moments (5 - 15mins relying upon the heap) so it can react to subsequent requests without a cold start.

Chapter # 32

AWS CloudFront

CloudFront is Amazon's worldwide substance delivery network with enormous limits and scale. It is advanced for execution and adaptability. Security features are additionally implicit and you can design them for the ideal assistance. The client is responsible for the service and can make changes on the fly. It incorporates ongoing detailing so you can screen the performance and make changes to the application or the way the CDN interfaces with your application. It has been upgraded for static and dynamic items and video delivery.

To configure CloudFront first you need to make a CloudFront circulation so that CloudFront realizes where to convey the substance from. You specify source servers (S3 cans or HTTP servers) to store your articles (documents). You transfer the documents which can be site pages, pictures and media records to your starting point servers. At that point, you make the distributions so that CloudFront knows which beginning servers to get the records from. You can also determine whether you need to log all solicitations and whether you need to empower the circulation when it is made. CloudFront relegates a space name to your distribution which you can find in the support. CloudFront will send the arrangement of the distribution to the entirety of its edge areas.

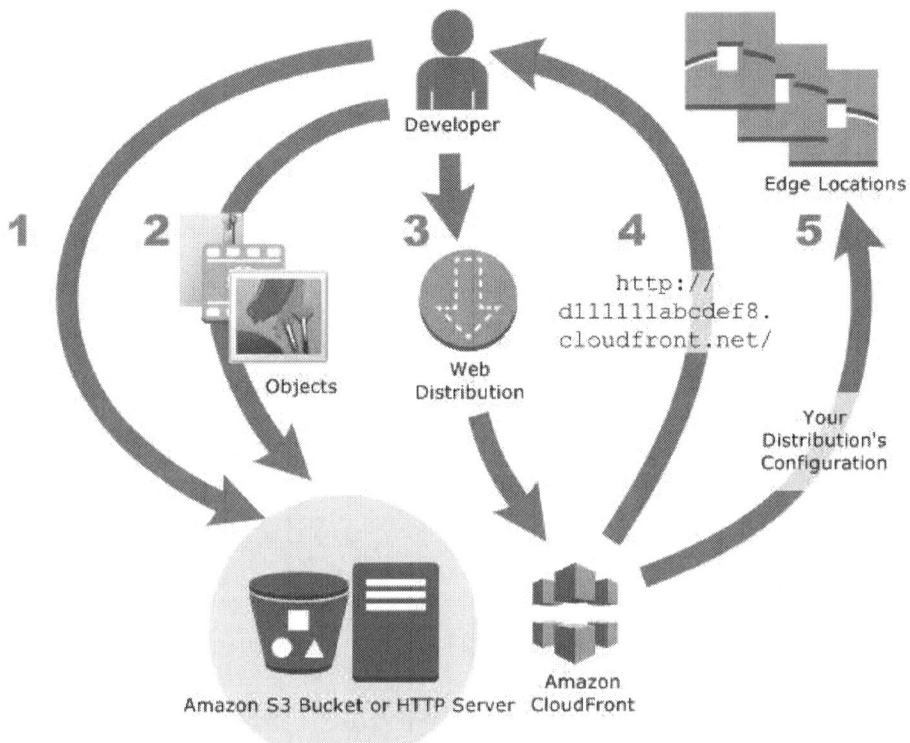

At the point when a client demands questions on your site or application, the DNS courses the request to the closest CloudFront edge area, which can best serve the client's request in terms of latency. In the edge area, CloudFront will check the store to check whether the substance being mentioned is there in the reserve and returns it to the client. If the substance isn't there in the store, at that point CloudFront will advance the request to the appropriate starting point server. The origin server will send the comparing record to the CloudFront edge area which will be sent by CloudFront to the client and furthermore put away in the reserve in the event that another person attempts to demand that document.

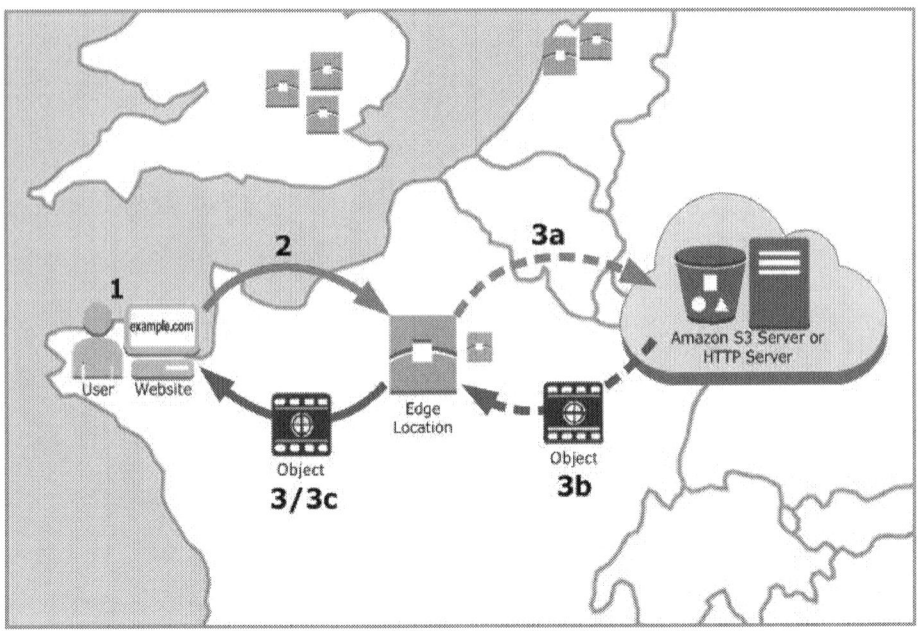

CloudFront guarantees that information is worldwide distributed with the best possible performance. We can ensure our substance by utilizing CloudFront's private element to manage who can get to our substance. CloudFront is one of the most effortless and exceptionally accessible content delivery networks in the market.

Behaviors

Behaviors are the place you can do every one of the setups. It enables you to enforce approaches, change or shift the kind of content being conveyed relying upon who's mentioning it or to what extent an item will remain in-store. CloudFront Distributions have one to numerous Behaviors, there's constantly one default Behavior. You can have different Behavior arranged by priority and if in a specific order of priority no condition is met, at that point the default Behavior will happen.

Restrictions, Errors, and Tags

CloudFront enables you to restrict access based on the geological area of the requester at no extra expenses. You can either white-list or boycott an area. This could be because of security reasons or because of the way that you just reserve the privileges to appropriate content to a couple of districts. Errors enable you to restore a mistake page when there is a mistake. You can reserve the error page for a specific measure of time and furthermore set the reaction code that should be sent.

Distributions

Distributions are the launch of CloudFront. It goes about as a pointer to the original content that you are facilitating either in an AWS or custom beginning. The sources should be indicated in the appropriation so that

CloudFront realizes where to get the content when a request comes in and we don't have the content put away in the cache.

Chapter # 33

Cloud Computing on AWS:

Distributed computing is the on-demand delivery of register control, database storage, applications, and other IT assets through a cloud services stage by means of the Internet with pay-as-you-go pricing. Regardless of whether you are running applications that offer photographs to a great many mobile clients or you're supporting the basic tasks of your business, a cloud services stage gives quick access to adaptable and ease IT assets. With distributed computing, you don't have to make huge upfront interests in equipment and invest a great deal of energy in the truly difficult work of dealing with that hardware. Rather, you can arrangement precisely the correct sort and size of computing assets you have to control your newest brilliant thought or work your IT office. You can access the same number of assets as you need, instantly, and pay for what you use. Utilizing distributed computing, associations can utilize shared processing and capacity assets as opposed to building, working, and improving foundation all alone. Cloud computing gives a basic method to get to servers, storage, databases and an expansive arrangement of use benefits over the Internet. A cloud services platform, for example, Amazon Web Services claims and keeps up the system associated equipment required for these application services, while you arrangement and use what you need through a web application.

- Cloud computing is a model that empowers the accompanying highlights.

- Users can arrangement and release assets on-request.

- Resources can be scaled up or down consequently, depends on the load

- Resources are open over a system with legitimate security.

Cloud service organizations can empower a compensation as-you-go model, where clients are charged dependent on the kind of assets and per utilization.

How Does Cloud Computing Work?

To understand the operations of a cloud framework, it is simpler to easier it into two areas: the front end and the back end. They are associated with one another through a system, for the most part, the Internet. The front end is the side of the PC client or customer. The back end is 'the cloud' area of the framework.

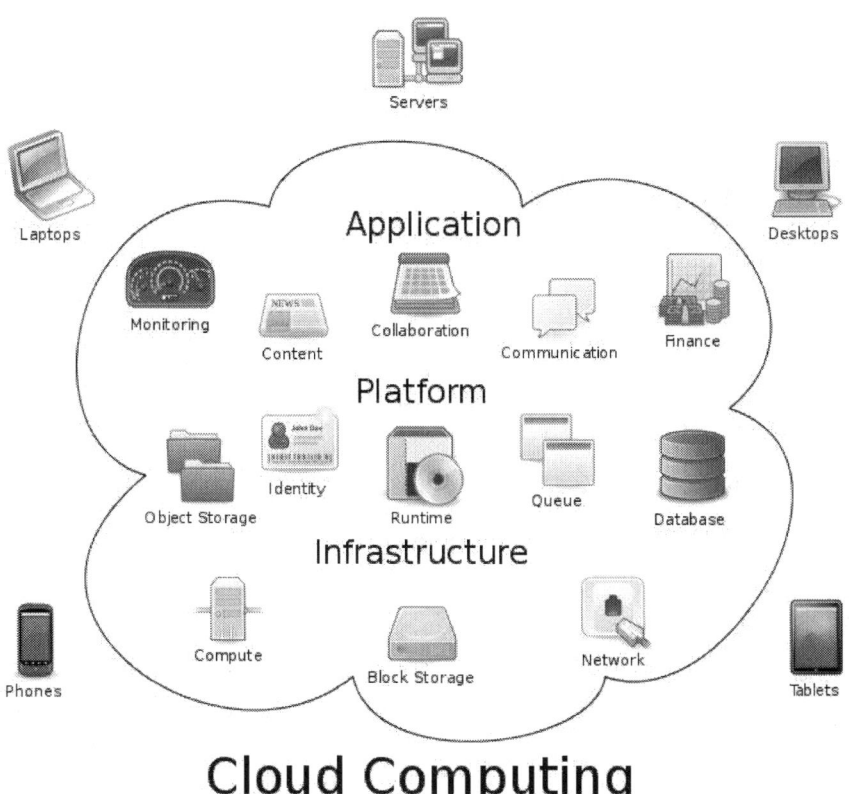

The front end comprises the customer's PC or computer network. Also the application basic to get to the cloud computing framework. It isn't fundamental that all cloud computing frameworks have a similar UI. Toward the back of the cloud innovation framework, there are different PCs, servers and information storage frameworks that make up the cloud. A cloud computing framework might incorporate any PC program, from information handling to video games. Normally every application has its own server which is dedicated.

Types of Clouds

There are three kinds of clouds — Public, Private, and Hybrid cloud.

Public Cloud

In the public cloud, third-party organizations make assets and services accessible to their clients by means of the Internet. Client's information and related security are with the service providers' possessed framework.

Private Cloud

A private cloud also gives practically comparable features as open cloud, however, the information and services are managed by the association or by the outsider just for the client's association. In this sort of cloud, significant control is over the foundation so security-related issues are limited.

Hybrid Cloud

A hybrid cloud is the mix of both private and open cloud. The choice to run on the private or open cloud, for the most part, relies upon different parameters like affectability of information and applications, industry certifications and required measures, guidelines, and so on.

Cloud Service Models

There are three sorts of service models in the cloud – IaaS, PaaS, and SaaS.

IaaS

IaaS represents Infrastructure as a Service. It gives clients the capacity to arrangement preparing, storage, and system availability on request. Utilizing this service model, the clients can build up their own applications on these assets.

PaaS

PaaS represents the Platform as a Service. Here, the service organization gives different services like databases, lines, workflow engines, e-mails, and so forth to their clients. The client would then be able to utilize these parts for building their own applications. The services, accessibility of assets and information backup are dealt with by the service provider that encourages the clients to concentrate more on their application's usefulness.

SaaS

SaaS represents Software as a Service. As the name proposes, here the third-party providers give end-client applications to their clients with some managerial capacity at the application level, for example, the capacity to make and deal with their clients. Additionally, some degree of adaptability is conceivable, for example, the clients can utilize their own corporate logos, colors, and so forth.

Advantages of Cloud Computing

Here is a list of the absolute most significant preferences that Cloud Computing brings to the table:

- **Cost-Efficient** – Building our own servers and instruments is time-consuming just as costly as we have to arrange, pay for, introduce, and design costly equipment, sometime before we need it. However, utilizing cloud computing, we pay for the sum we use and when we utilize the computing assets. As such, cloud computing is cost proficient.

- **Reliability** – A cloud computing stage gives significantly more managed, solid and steady help than an in-house IT foundation. It ensures 24x7 and 365 days of administration. On the off chance that any of the servers fizzles, at that point hosted applications and services can without much of a stretch be transited to any of the accessible servers.

- **Unlimited Storage** – Cloud computing gives practically boundless storage limits, i.e., we need not stress over coming up short on an extra room or expanding our present extra room accessibility. We can access to such an extent or as small as we need.

- **Backup and Recovery** – Storing information in the cloud, backing it up and reestablishing the equivalent is generally simpler than putting away it on a physical device. The cloud service providers also have enough innovation to recuperate our information, so there is the comfort of recovering our information whenever.

- **Easy Access to Information** – Once you register yourself in the cloud, you can get to your record from anyplace on the planet gave there is web association by then. There are different storage and security facilities that vary with the record type picked.

Disadvantages of Cloud Computing

Although Cloud Computing gives a great arrangement of favorable circumstances, it has a few downsides also that frequently bring up issues about its productivity.

Security issues

Security is a significant issue in cloud computing. The cloud service providers execute the best security standards and industry certifications, in any case, putting away information and sign documents on outer service providers consistently bear a hazard.

AWS cloud framework is intended to be the most adaptable and verified cloud arrange. It gives adaptable and highly dependable stage that empowers clients to send applications and information rapidly and safely.

Technical issues

As cloud service providers offer administrations to a number of customers every day, here and there the framework can have some significant issues prompting business forms incidentally being suspended. Furthermore, if the web association is disconnected, at that point we won't have the option to get to any of the applications, servers, or information from the cloud.

Security

Cloud security at AWS is the highest priority. As an AWS client, you will profit by a server farm and system design worked to meet the requirements of the most security-touchy associations. Security in the cloud is a lot of like security in your on-premises server farms just without the expenses of keeping up offices and equipment. In the cloud, you don't need to oversee physical servers or storage devices. Rather, you use programming based security tools to screen and ensure the progression of data into and of out of your cloud assets.

An advantage of the AWS Cloud is that it enables you to scale and develop while keeping up a protected domain and paying just for the services you use. This means you can have the security you need at a lower cost than in an on-premises condition.

As an AWS client, you acquire all the accepted procedures of AWS approaches, design, and operational procedures worked to fulfill the requirements of our most security-sensitive clients. Get the adaptability and agility you need in security controls.

The AWS Cloud empowers a mutual obligation model. While AWS oversees the security of the cloud, you are responsible for security in the cloud. This means you hold control of the security you decide to execute to ensure your very own content, stage, applications, frameworks, and systems no uniquely in contrast to you would in an on a location server farm.

AWS gives you direction and skill through online resources, personnel, and accomplices. AWS gives you warnings for current issues, in addition to you have the chance to work with AWS when you experience security issues.

You gain access to many devices and features to assist you in meeting your security goals. AWS gives security-explicit devices and features across system security, design the executives, get to control, and information encryption.

Chapter # 34

Cloud Storage

Cloud storage is a cloud computing model that stores information on the Internet through a cloud computing supplier who manages and works information storage as assistance. It's conveyed on request within the nick of a time limit and costs and wipes out purchasing and dealing with your very own information storage framework. This gives you agility, worldwide scale, and strength, with "whenever anyplace" data access.

How Does Cloud Storage Work?

Cloud storage is acquired from a third-party cloud purchaser who owns and works information storage limits and conveys it over the Internet in a compensation as-you-go model. These cloud storage merchants oversee limit, security, and durability to make information open to your applications all around the world.

Applications get to distributed storage through conventional storage conventions or legitimately by means of an API. Numerous sellers offer corresponding administrations intended to help gather, oversee, verify and examine the information at a massive scale.

Advantages of Cloud Storage

Storing information in the cloud gives IT offices a chance to change three regions:

1. **Total Cost of Ownership.** With cloud storage, there are no equipment to buy, storage to the arrangement, or capital being utilized for "sometime in the not so distant future" situations. You can include or remove limit request, rapidly change execution and maintenance qualities, and pay for capacity that you really use. Less as often as possible got to information can even be consequently moved to bring down cost levels as per auditable principles, driving economies of scale.

2. **Time to Deployment.** At the point when advancement groups are prepared to execute, infrastructure should never back them off. Cloud storage enables IT to rapidly convey the accurate measure of capacity required, right when it's

required. This enables IT to concentrate on handling complex application issues as opposed to managing storage frameworks.

3. **Information Management.** Concentrating storage in the cloud makes an enormous influence point for new use cases. By utilizing cloud storage lifecycle the executive's strategies, you can perform incredible data the management tasks including computerized tiering or securing down information backing of compliance requirements.

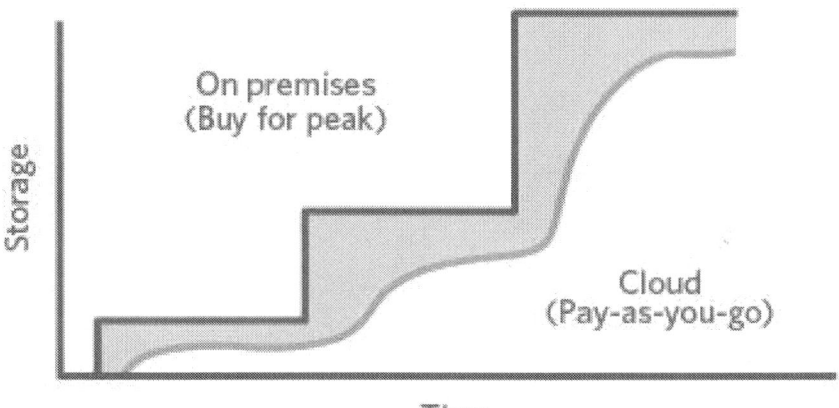

Cloud storage Requirements

Guaranteeing your organization's basic information is protected, secure, and accessible when required is basic. There are a few major requirements when considering putting away information in the cloud.

Durability. Information should be repetitively put away, in a perfect world over numerous offices and various devices in every office. Catastrophic events, human blunder, or mechanical flaws should not bring about information loss.

Availability. All information should be accessible when required, yet there is a distinction between archives and production information. The perfect cloud storage will convey the correct parity of recovery times and costs.

Security. All information is ideally encrypted, both very still and in travel. Authorizations and access controls should work similarly too in the cloud as they accomplish for on-premises storage.

Types of Cloud Storage

There are three sorts of cloud information storage: object storage, record storage, and block storage. Each offers its own favorable circumstances and have their very own utilization cases:

1. **Object Storage -** Applications created in the cloud frequently exploit object storage's immense scalability and metadata attributes. Article storage arrangements like Amazon Simple Storage Service (S3) are perfect for building current applications without any preparation that require scale and adaptability, and can also be utilized to import existing information stores for investigation, reinforcement, or archive.

2. **File Storage -** Some applications need to get to shared records and require a document framework. This kind of capacity is regularly supported by a Network Attached Storage (NAS) server. Document storage arrangements like Amazon Elastic File System (EFS) are perfect for use cases like enormous content repositories,

advancement situations, media stores, or client home indexes.

3. **Block Storage -** Other project applications like databases or ERP frameworks frequently require committed, low dormancy storage for each host. This is analogous to coordinate direct-attached storage (DAS) or a Storage Area Network (SAN). Square-based cloud storage arrangements like Amazon Elastic Block Store (EBS) are provisioned with each virtual server and offer the ultra-low dormancy required for high-performance tasks at hand.

Hybrid Cloud Storage

Numerous clients need to exploit the advantages of cloud storage, yet have applications running on-premises that require low-inertness access to their information, or need quick information move to the cloud. AWS hybrid cloud storage structures associate your on-premises applications and frameworks to cloud storage to assist you with decreasing costs, limit the board trouble, and improve with your information. AWS hybrid storage, move and relocation administrations incorporate flawlessly with applications utilizing standard conventions, relieve WAN latencies, and give a predictable AWS the management experience.

Cloud storage Service Details

Amazon Elastic Block Store

Amazon Elastic Block Store (Amazon EBS) gives exceptionally accessible, reliable, low-inactivity block storage for Amazon EC2. It encourages you to tune applications with the correct storage limit, execution, and cost. EBS is intended for workloads that require determined stockpiling available by single EC2 occurrences. Run of the mill use cases incorporate social and NoSQL databases (like Microsoft SQL Server and MySQL or Cassandra and MongoDB), Big Data analytics engine (like the Hadoop/HDFS biological system and Amazon EMR), stream and log handling applications (like Kafka and Splunk), and data warehousing applications (like Vertica and Teradata).

Amazon S3

Amazon Simple Storage Service (Amazon S3) is object storage intended to store and access any kind of information over the Internet. It is secure,

99.999999999% strong, and scales past several trillions of articles. S3 is utilized for recovery and backup, tiered archive, client-driven content (like photographs, recordings, music, and documents), information lakes for Big Data examination and data warehouse platforms, or as an establishment for serverless processing plan.

Amazon FSx for Luster

Amazon FSx for Luster is a completely managed document framework that is improved for compute-intensive workloads, such as high-performance computing, AI, and media information handling work processes. With Amazon FSx, you can dispatch and run a Luster record framework that can procedure enormous informational collections at up to many gigabytes every second of throughput, a large number of IOPS, and sub-millisecond latencies.

Amazon FSx for Luster is flawlessly coordinated with Amazon S3, making it simple to connect your long-term informational indexes with your high-performance file systems to run compute-intensive workloads.

Chapter # 35

AWS Limitations

AWS is the quickest developing Cloud supplier, and it offers in excess of 70 unique administrations. For pretty much any assistance that you could consider, there is most likely effectively a specific help on AWS where you can convey your arrangement. And, the whole AWS infrastructure is available to you.

In any case, this doesn't imply that you can actually do anything you desire. A portion of the AWS restrictions are self-evident, yet others are covered up and should be deliberately considered before you begin.

How about we investigate a portion of these limitations and how you can defeat them and guard your business in the AWS world.

1. AWS service limits

AWS administration limits are set by the stage. The confinements are there to:

- Prevent you from spending an excess of cash on your first experience with the stage

- Protect the framework itself from uncontrolled asset utilization

One of the principal features of all Cloud frameworks, including AWS, is adaptability and the capacity to build assets up when vital. All in all, what's the issue?

The appropriate response is very simple. You don't generally require that numerous assets. A large portion of the organizations doesn't have to have in excess of five Elastic IPs for every district or more than 20 EC2 occurrences for each locale. The default limitations are set dependent on the necessities of a normal client. Increment these and you'll pay more.

Fortunately, you can present a request for a bigger number of assets if you truly need in excess of five Elastic IP addresses for every locale.

AWS places default restrains on a few basic assets. These include:

- EC2 Instance: Default Limit: 20 for every district

- EBS Volume: Default Limit: 5,000 volumes or total size of 20 TiB

- Elastic IP: Default Limit: 5 for every district

- Elastic Load Balancer: Default Limit: 10

- High I/O Instance: Default Limit: 2

- Virtual Private Cloud: Default Limit: 5

These limits are frequently called soft limitations since you can also demand fewer assets if you wish.

There are additionally hard AWS limitations that cannot be changed by any means. The accompanying areas have hard constraints:

- EC2 Security Groups (EC2 Classic): Maximum of 500 for every example and every Security Group can have a limit of 100 rules/permissions

- EC2 Security Groups (EC2-VPC): Up to 100 security bunches for every VPC

As should be obvious, these limits are identified with security issues. Since security is one of the key issues in Cloud computing, you should trust in your Cloud supplier around there. You can see the full list of AWS restrictions on the authority AWS administration limits page.

2. Technology limitations

An outstanding trait of this restricting element is that it very well may be applied to all Cloud services, not simply on AWS. It relies upon the general innovation advancement that cannot be immediately settled. Give me a chance to clarify with a model. You have chosen to make a transport service that individuals can utilize on the web. To transport myself, I should simply sign in to the application, pick the area, and click "Go!" There's only one catch. This service can't really work since, you got it, and transporting innovation hasn't been grown at this point (unfortunately).

Truly, my model is somewhat extraordinary, however, you get the thought. If it isn't feasible for Amazon SES (Simple Email Service) to send more than 1 email for each second (in the sandbox condition), there is no reason for requesting an expansion right now. Innovation is building up every day, and it will unquestionably be conceivable to send 100 messages for each second utilizing Amazon SES eventually. It's simply not feasible at the present time.

The most ideal approach to ensure your business against such limitations is to know about them. Thus, ensure you have all the important data before you make an unreasonable request. It's a lot simpler to work around technical limitations than attempting to fix them.

3. Lack of relevant knowledge by your team

If you decide to work with AWS as your Cloud supplier, be set up to learn and put resources into your group's instruction. As we referenced previously, AWS is a phenomenal and broad stage, and you have to understand what you're doing if you need to utilize it. To have the option to exploit all the helpful features and services offered by AWS, you'll need to know the platform as deeply as possible.

To effectively deal with your AWS stage, you should put resources into your group. It is in every case great to employ an experienced engineer who has just worked with AWS, however, you should also enable your group to learn as much as they can about the stage. There is a lot of assets that they can use, from the rich AWS Docs area, network sites, and teams, to web-based learning stages.

It is in every case great to finish the training procedure with accreditation, so make a point to urge your colleagues to step advance and get AWS guaranteed.

4. Specialized support expense

At the point when I state that specialized help is an AWS limitation, I'm not referring to untrained staff. I'm referring to the extra costs that devoted technical support requires.

Just, all things considered, your month to month charge incorporates a restricted measure of help. If you need prompt help you can select one of three help bundles: Developer, Business, or Enterprise. While this will build your month to month costs, it's additionally an investment that guarantees that you will have the top group available to you if there should arise an occurrence of an emergency.

Here is a depiction of AWS's pricing for help:

- Developer: $29/month

- Business: Greater of $100 – or –

10% of month to month AWS use for the first $0–$10K

7% of month to month AWS utilization from $10K–$80K

5% of month to month AWS utilization from $80K–$250K

3% of month to month AWS utilization over $250K

- Enterprise: Greater of $15,000 – or –

10% of month to month AWS utilization for the first $0–$150K

7% of month to month AWS utilization from $150K–$500K

5% of month to month AWS utilization from $500K–$1M

3% of month to month AWS utilization over $1M

There are two things that you can do to overcome this limitation:

- Be arranged for extra expenses and add them to your general costs of doing business

- Find your own AWS Consulting Partner

Chapter # 36

How to Make Money with Amazon

There are various ways that you can profit with Amazon, and in this article, we'll investigate ten of the present potential outcomes. Almost certainly, much more conceivable outcomes will emerge sooner rather than later.

1. Amazon Associates

Amazon Associates is Amazon's name for its partner program. You can sign up Amazon Associates and use subsidiary links to send guests to Amazon, and if the guest causes a buy you'll to gain a referral commission.

Amazon was one of the pioneers of the affiliate industry and theirs is as yet one of the most (if not the most) well-known partner programs on the planet. With such a large number of various items being sold on Amazon, you can advance pretty much anything you can consider.

One of the advantages of member advertising is that you won't have to manage things like stock, upfront expenses, and client support.

The commission that you'll win will vary depending upon the class of the item that is acquired, however by and large it is around 4%. This may appear to be a low rate, yet remember that Amazon changes over a high level of guests into purchasers on the grounds that such a significant number of individuals are as of now loyal clients. Also, the guest doesn't have to buy the definite item that you are advancing. After they click your affiliate link, you'll procure commissions on any item they buy from Amazon during the following 24 hours. This is extraordinary in light of the fact that numerous individuals will click your connection, and afterward end up purchasing something absolutely irrelevant. Regardless you procure a commission for it!

Amazon Associates can be utilized with sites and web journals that spread pretty much at any point (make certain to read their terms when you're joining). Many individuals make specialty sites for the particular motivation behind profiting with Amazon Associates. Pretty much any blog can profit from Amazon Associates, so it's very worth some consideration if you as of now have your own site or blog. I've been an Amazon Associate for quite a while now. The cash I make as an affiliate doesn't make up a big level of my general pay, however, I do get paid two or three hundred dollars consistently. And, one of the decent things is, I haven't done a lot to earn this. The majority of my referrals originate from a blog that has some incidental connections at whatever point an item is referenced in the blog content.

2. Sell Retail Arbitrage

Retail Arbitrage includes purchasing items at one retail location (or site) and exchanging them for benefit. With this plan of action, you'll discover extraordinary arrangements at an assortment or retail locations and sites and research to perceive the amount you can sell a similar item for on Amazon. In case you're ready to sell it for a good benefit you purchase the deal or limited thing and afterward show is available to be purchased on Amazon. If you realize how to do it, a retail exchange can be an incredible plan of action. The issue is that it includes an expectation to learn and adapt, and in the event that you don't have the foggiest idea what you're doing you can lose a decent piece of cash all the while.

3. Sell Private Label Products

Private marking includes making your own image. You'll have a producer who makes items with your logo and brand name on them. This is a mainstream approach, and this is the means by which my better half and I manufactured a six-figure business rapidly.

There are a few motivations to cherish selling private name items on Amazon:

1. There are a lot of makers who will make items for you, so you can even maintain this business directly from your home.

2. Amazon will satisfy the entirety of the requests for you through their FBA program, which implies you don't need to manage shipments to clients or returns.

3. By outsourcing both the manufacturing and satisfaction, this can be a for the most part without hands business.

4. Your small locally established business can resemble a bigger organization to clients.

5. There are unlimited possibilities. You can make any sort of item you can envision.

6. Once you have one successful item, you can copy the procedure and add other new items to increase your image.

7. Unlike the retail exchange model, you won't have to continually look for incredible arrangements on items that you can exchange.

4. Sell Used Items

While you can sell new things on Amazon, you can also sell utilized things (barring a few classes that don't permit utilized items). Numerous individuals make a decent pay by purchasing modest things at swap meets, yard deals, second-hand shops, and sell-offs, and afterward exchanging them for a benefit at locales like Amazon and eBay.

5. Compose and Sell Books and EBooks

If you like to compose, perhaps the most ideal approaches to make cash is to sell books or digital books on Amazon. With Amazon's Kindle program it's exceptionally simple to make and sell your own digital book on any subject that you can imagine.

It's conceivable to profit with Kindle with or without your very own current crowd. Obviously, if you as of now have a blog or email list that you can use to help get your book launched rapidly, that will help.

6. Merchandise by Amazon

Merchandise by Amazon is an incredible open door for designers or any individual who is happy to re-appropriate plan work. Through this program, you can transfer your very own structures and select the items that you need to sell (like shirts for instance). At the point when somebody buys your thing, Amazon will deal with creation, transportation, and client support and you'll get paid.

With this plan of action, you won't need to manage stock and you'll have no upfront expenses? Regardless you'll have command over the valuing and the careful items that you sell.

7. Amazon Flex Delivery

With Amazon Flex you can make $18 – $25 every hour conveying bundles to clients. The best part is that you can set your own timetable and working hours. Flex is at present accessible in 50 urban communities, however, I imagine that number is probably going to grow before long.

8. Amazon Home Services

Have you at any point known about Amazon Home Services? I hadn't, up to this point. Through Amazon Home Services clients can get services like housekeeping, furniture gets together, jack of all trades services, yard cutting, and that's only the tip of the iceberg. It's hard to believe, but it's true. You can pay Amazon to have your grass cut.

That means there are open doors for individuals like you and me to give these services and profit. You can become familiar with the open door here.

There is an application procedure that you'll have to experience, yet once you are affirmed Amazon will send you work. You'll require general obligation protection, and in case you're an exchange proficient (like a plumber or electrician) you'll be authorized.

Chapter # 37

Common Troubleshooting

Regardless of whether you are simply learning AWS or have been utilizing the amazon web services for quite a while, you will invariably run into availability issues in your arrangements. For instance, not ready to SSH into the EC2 example, the application level can't converse with the database, etc. In fact, there might be times when the availability was working fine when your stack was deployed, however it broke after some time. I am certain you can identify with probably a portion of these experiences. In this post, I will discuss how to investigate and resolve a portion of the usually experienced availability issues in AWS arrangements.

Utilizing Telnet for Port Check

Before we start discussing the issues, it allows first to become familiar with a basic system named port watch that can be utilized for investigating. In networking, a port check refers to testing whether a port on a given node is tuning in or not. For instance, in the event that you need to check for the standard SSH port on a machine, you would check port 22. For what reason is a port check significant? It is significant in light of the fact that it is one of the most principal checks you can accomplish for testing availability between two segments without thinking a lot about the segments themselves. To clarify this further, if an application running on an EC2 example is neglecting to associate with the RDS case and the port check for the database port fails from the EC2 occasion, you can without much of an easily confirm that there is some network issue between these two.

You can utilize the telnet utility for a port check. It is accessible on most stages and is frequently pre-introduced or can be effectively introduced at a later point. So as to do the port check, you will determine an order like the one demonstrated as follows.

telnet <target-ip-address-or-dns-name> <port>

If you can telnet effectively, the port check is successful. Else, it has failed. Simple!

The accompanying screen capture shows a successful port check utilizing telnet on an EC2 occasion with the IP address 10.1.0.195 on the SSH port 22.

```
[ec2-user@ip-10-0-0-60 ~]$ telnet 10.1.0.195 22
Trying 10.1.0.195...
Connected to 10.1.0.195.
Escape character is '^]'.
SSH-2.0-OpenSSH_7.4
```

Here is another screen capture that shows a failed port check. For this situation, the telnet association has just hung (that is, it can't interface effectively). In any case, you may see different variations like not ready to interface, and so on.

```
[ec2-user@ip-10-0-0-60 ~]$ telnet 10.1.0.196 9090
Trying 10.1.0.196...
```

Common Connectivity Issues in AWS Deployments

We should discuss some basic availability issues in AWS organizations now. Here is a list of such issues.

- Not ready to associate with an EC2 occurrence by means of SSH.

- An application running on an EC2 example can't associate with the RDS occurrence.

- The clients are not ready to get to the web application.

These are only a portion of the usually experienced issues. However, these speak to some normally watched examples and you may discover different issues that pursue a similar example.

In any case, if the port check failed, the accompanying could be some normal reasons.

- **Use of incorrect IP address or DNS name for the EC2 occurrence:** This can occur because of a client mistake or the EC2 case was rebooted and it's open IP and DNS name changed. Presently, in the event that you have appointed an Elastic IP to the example, it won't change upon reboot. However, Elastic IPs are costly and utilized uniquely for significant occurrences regularly. In this way, make a point to check the IP/DNS name is right.

- **A Firewall is obstructing the SSH association:** At times, the corporate InfoSec group may square SSH availability to open IP addresses. This is regularly done to avoid the situation where a programmer can exploit an SSL vulnerability to hack into the corporate system. You can regularly do some underlying investigating for this by utilizing the SSH verbose choice (- v or - vvv) while setting up the SSH association. In the event that that is the situation, you should work with your InfoSec group on the goals. One potential arrangement is to assign out an Elastic IP to your EC2 case and get a special case from them to permit SSH to this IP address. Another potential firewall issue could be the OS firewall is hindering the SSH association, (for example, the iptables setup). To fix this you should alter the firewall design (ideally) or turn the firewall off.

An application running on an EC2 occasion can't associate with the RDS example

To investigate this further, you can do a port check from the EC2 case to the RDS occurrence port and check whether that works.

The accompanying screen capture shows a successful telnet port check to an RDS occurrence.

```
[ec2-user@ip-10-0-0-60 ~]$ telnet c9appsdb.cbprpfefv5tt.us-east-1.rds.amazonaws.
com 3306
Trying 10.0.2.135...
Connected to c9appsdb.cbprpfefv5tt.us-east-1.rds.amazonaws.com.
Escape character is '^]'.
J
5.6.39k?5,{LHe?Da;E(6ul@;F,mysql_native_password
```

All things considered, check for the accompanying.

- **Use of erroneous RDS case name or port:** Check your application setup to check whether it has the right RDS occurrence name and port worth. If the port check failed, these could be some normal reasons.

- **Use of incorrect RDS occurrence name or port:** Double-check the example name and port to guarantee these are right.

- **Is the RDS case up? RDS bolsters the shutdown of occurrences.** This is regularly valuable for cost control purposes when the occasion isn't being used. For instance, closing down an improvement RDS case during the ends of the week. In this way, check if the RDS occurrence is accessible.

- **Incorrect Security Group arrangement:** Check whether the Security Group appointed to the RDS occurrence has right entrance rules to allow network from the EC2 occasion. This would commonly include guaranteeing the entrance rule has the right source subnet (which should be your EC2 subnet) and target (database) port indicated. The accompanying screen capture shows entrance rule sections for MySQL/Aurora RDS case.

	Summary	Inbound Rules	Outbound Rules	Tags

Edit

Type	Protocol	Port Range	Source	Description
MySQL/Aurora (3306)	TCP (6)	3306	10.0.0.0/16	
MySQL/Aurora (3306)	TCP (6)	3306	10.1.0.0/16	
MySQL/Aurora (3306)	TCP (6)	3306	10.2.0.0/16	

FAQs

Q: What is the AWS Resource Access Manager?

An: AWS Resource Access Manager (RAM) gives you the capacity to safely share your assets crosswise over AWS accounts or inside your Organization. You can now centrally secure assets and use RAM to impart assets to different records, eliminating the need for an arrangement and manage assets in each record. At the point when you share an asset with another record, that record is allowed access to the asset and any approaches and consents in that record will apply to the common asset.

Q: What sorts of AWS assets would I be able to share utilizing RAM?

An: The list of assets you can impart to RAM is recorded in the shareable assets segment of the RAM client control.

Q: How would I get started with RAM?

An: You can begin with RAM by making a Resource Share utilizing the API/CLI or the AWS Management Console. You can easily share assets by adding assets and records to a Resource Share. Resource Share awards accounts for access to assets.

Q: Who can I share resources with?

An: You can share assets to any AWS account, and id you are a piece of AWS Organizations, at that point you can also share resources to Organizational Units (OUs) or your whole Organization. If you share assets with accounts that are outside of your organization, at that point those records will get an invitation to the Resource Share and can begin utilizing the mutual assets after accepting the invitation.

Q: How can I view resources that have been shared with my record?

An: You can see assets that have been shared with your record in the RAM reassure or by utilizing the RAM APIs. The assets that have been shared with your record will also show up in the separate asset reassure pages and the individual List/Describe APIs for those asset types. For instance, when an AWS Deliverator Rule is shared to a record then that standard will show up on the Deliverator page of the Amazon Route53 reassure alongside different guidelines claimed by that record and the common principle will also be returned in the reaction of the ListDelivertorRules API.

Q: Will I bring about any charges for sharing my assets to different records?

An: No. You can share assets at no extra cost.

Q: Can I tag a Resource Share?

An: Indeed, you can tag a Resource Share at the hour of creation or whenever after creation.

Q: How can I control access to resources shared with me?

An: You can determine IAM arrangements to control access to assets shared with you.

Conclusion:

In the present market center, where each procedure is turning out to be increasingly mechanical and each association is going to cloud services, being prepared in AWS is an advantage bit of leeway for you. A few huge associations require people who are talented in cloud computing services so as to change and scale up their organizations. Being prepared and ensured in AWS won't just assist the person with validating their cloud abilities and advance further in the association, yet additionally benefits the association by having somebody capable in cloud services information as opposed to by somebody who isn't prepared in it. With innovation growing always, it is imperative to be continually fully informed regarding your insight and practice on AWS. For this, it is significant that you pick an instructional class that isn't fixed with a specific time and is fairly continually developing after some time. You can discover the absolute best certifications for AWS preparing in Bangalore. Certification in AWS will help advantage you to look over a wide scope of career choices, for example, AWS arrangements designer, AWS engineer, cloud planner, DevOps Engineer, and some more. A decent AWS course shows you how to plan, and scale AWS Cloud implementations, moreover the prescribed procedures suggested by Amazon.

A dominant part of the world piece of the overall industry is moving towards cloud computing and their first decision is AWS. Some well-known MNCs who have gone to AWS are Netflix, Kelloggs, General Electric and Adobe.

Cloud computing is a sticky business one needs to keep proceeding with except if something very unfortunate occurs and the organization/individual needs to change to some other organization. AWS conveys a promising cloud service that is capable of you for the lifetime. You won't need to go through years and a large number of dollars over between cloud moves for AWS Cloud Services won't grant you any discouragement. It will give you a chance to keep your client connection flawless and blooming through its consistent services, obtaining its own prosperity.

Manufactured by Amazon.ca
Bolton, ON